The Complete Body Opponent Bag Book

by
Sammy Franco

Also by Sammy Franco:

Heavy Bag Training: Boxing, Mixed Martial Arts & Self-Defense
Gun Safety: For Home Defense and Concealed Carry
Out of the Cage: A Complete Guide to Beating a Mixed Martial Artist on the Street
Warrior Wisdom: Inspiring Ideas from the World's Greatest Warriors
Judge, Jury and Executioner
Savage Street Fighting: Tactical Savagery as a Last Resort
Feral Fighting: Level 2 WidowMaker
Ground War: How to Destroy a Grappler in a Street Fight
The Combat Conditioning Workout Journal
War Blade: A Complete Guide to Tactical Knife Fighting
The WidowMaker Program: Maximum Punishment for Extreme Situations
War Craft: Street Fighting Tactics of the War Machine
War Machine: How to Transform Yourself Into a Vicious and Deadly Street Fighter
The Bigger They Are, The Harder They Fall: How to Defeat a Larger & Stronger
Adversary in a Street Fight
First Strike: Mastering the Preemptive Strike for Street Combat
1001 Street Fighting Secrets: The Principles of Contemporary Fighting Arts
When Seconds Count: Everyone's Guide to Self-Defense
Killer Instinct: Unarmed Combat for Street Survival
Street Lethal: Unarmed Urban Combat

The Complete Body Opponent Bag Book
Copyright © 2014 by Sammy Franco
ISBN 978-0-9853472-4-6
Printed in the United States of America

Published by Contemporary Fighting Arts, LLC.
P.O. Box 84028
Gaithersburg, Maryland 20883 USA
Phone: (301) 279-2244
Visit us online at: www.sammyfranco.com

For author interviews or publicity information, please send inquiries in care of the publisher.

Visit our web site at: www.sammyfranco.com

Table of Contents

Preface

The body opponent bag is a popular piece of workout equipment, especially for those who practice martial arts and self-defense. Unfortunately, however, most people don't know how to get full use of this unique punching bag.

More often than not, they simply punch or kick the BOB without a care in the world. In most cases, they are failing to maximize the full utility of this lifelike punching bag.

As someone with over 30 years of martial arts training, I can tell you the body opponent bag has many hidden training features that develop explosive speed and power, improve your endurance, and strengthen your entire body.

The Complete Body Opponent Bag Book is the authoritative resource for mastering this lifelike punching bag. It's filled with detailed photographs, step-by-step instructions, and dozens of unique workout routines that will challenge you for years to come.

Whether you are a beginner, intermediate of advanced practitioner, The Complete Body Opponent Bag Book is an invaluable resource that you'll refer to again and again.

I wish you the best of luck in your training.

Sammy Franco
Founder & President
Contemporary Fighting Arts

Important!

The information and techniques in this book can be dangerous and could lead to serious injury. The author, publisher, and distributors of this book disclaim any liability from loss, injury, or damage, personal or otherwise, resulting from the information and procedures in this book. This book is for academic study only.

Before you begin any exercise program, including those suggested in this book, it is important to check with your physician to see whether you have any condition that might be aggravated by strenuous exercise.

CHAPTER ONE
Meet BOB

The body opponent bag or BOB is a unique punching bag that's favored among self-defense practitioners, kick boxers, and martial artists of all styles and backgrounds. The BOB, however, is also becoming very popular with the general public who wants to relieve stress, improve their overall fitness, and pick up a few fighting skills along the way.

With so many different types of punching bags on the market, it becomes a bit confusing as to exactly what distinguishes the body opponent bag from other punching bags. What are the benefits of working out on the body opponent bag? What are the drawbacks? Exactly how do you use this lifelike punching bag? All of these questions, plus much more will be answered in this book.

What is a Body Opponent Bag?

The body opponent bag is a self-standing lifelike punching bag designed to withstand tremendous punishment by allowing the practitioner to attack it with a wide variety of offensive techniques.

Essentially, the body opponent bag is made up of two parts: the torso and base. The torso is constructed of synthetic rubber material called plastisol and it can withstand tremendous abuse. In fact, my body opponent bag has been used daily for over fifteen years and it has never needed to be repaired or replaced.

The Torso

The torso of the body opponent bag is life-size, measuring approximately forty inches in height and twenty-three inches in width. While its interior is filled with durable, thick foam material. While the torso is durable and resistant to punches and kicks, it still can be punctured with sharp objects, so be careful when handling it.

The Base

The base of the body opponent bag is constructed of hollow, hard plastic and it serves four purposes. First, it provides the necessary support to hold the mannequin in place. Second, it allows you to adjust the torso at various height levels. Third, when filled with either water or sand, it provides the torso with the necessary weight and resistance. Finally, the base allows you to move and transport the bob easily.

Unlike the traditional heavy bag, the BOB is self-standing and doesn't need to be hung from the ceiling or affixed to a stand. This is particularly appealing to people who have limited space when training. When the base is completely filled, it will weigh approximately 270 pounds.

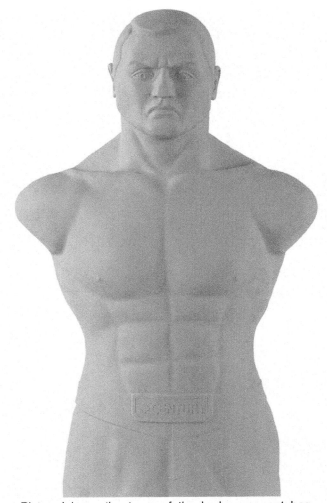

Pictured here, the torso of the body opponent bag. Notice its lifelike features.

"The body opponent bag is a unique punching bag with a broad appeal to many different types of consumers."

When most people think of a punching bag, the traditional heavy bag usually comes to mind.

The body opponent bag is just one of many types of punching bags on the market. For example, punching bags may also include: the double end bag, speed bag, upper cut bag, body snatcher bag as well as many others.

Pictured here, another type of self standing punching bag. Notice how the base is very similar to the one on the body opponent bag.

"Punching Bag" is a generic term that refers to a wide range of punching bags. For example, the double end bag is used for developing speed, timing, and fighting reflexes. This punching bag does have its purpose, but is doesn't hold a candle to the body opponent bag. In this photo, the author performs a horizontal elbow strike on the double end bag.

Benefits of BOB Training

The body opponent bag is a fantastic piece of training equipment that provides a wide range of benefits for the practitioner. In this section, I will discuss some of the many benefits that come from working out on the bag.

Developing Fighting Technique

The body opponent bag is a fantastic piece of equipment for developing your fighting skills and techniques. Compared to the traditional heavy bag, the BOB is a more specialized punching bag that develops a broader scope of self-defense techniques. So it's no surprise that self-defense practitioners, and martial artists of all styles and backgrounds regularly use the BOB for developing their particular style of fighting.

As you can imagine, a wide variety of kicks, punches, and strikes can be developed and ultimately perfected on the bag. However, the primary purpose of the BOB is to develop target accuracy for your striking techniques including jabs, crosses, hooks, uppercuts, elbow, and knee strikes.

There are, however, other fighting techniques that can be trained on the body opponent bag. Some include:

- Eye jabs

- Eye rakes
- Eye gouges
- Knife hand strikes
- Palm heels
- Bicep pops
- Head butts
- Hammer fists
- Tearing techniques
- Ground fighting skills
- Scenario based self-defense training
- Chokes and neck crank techniques

Developing Weapon Skills

Because of its lifelike features, the body opponent bag permits you to perform hand held weapons training. For example, you can practice stick strikes, knife attacks, kubotan techniques, and even pepper spray training on the bag. Just be certain to use the right equipment when training or you can permanently damage the bag.

Developing Fighting Attributes

Fighting attributes are unique qualities that enhance or amplify a particular fighting technique. They might include: speed, power, timing, agility, ambidexterity, coordination, combat conditioning as well as many others.

The body opponent bag is an ideal piece of equipment for developing some of these fighting attributes. They include some of the following:

- Proper Targeting
- Ambidexterity
- Offensive timing

- Balance and coordination
- Footwork skills
- Non-telegraphic movement
- Muscular relaxation

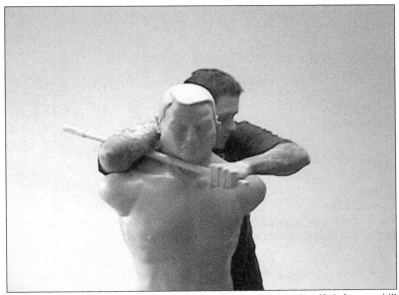

The body opponent bag is ideal for developing practical self-defense skills. Pictured here, the author performs a stick strangle on the BOB.

Fighting attributes are not just limited to the physical plane, there are mental and psychological fighting attributes that can be developed through consistent BOB training. They can include:

- Confidence
- Mental concentration
- Aggressiveness
- Psychological resilience
- Stress Reduction

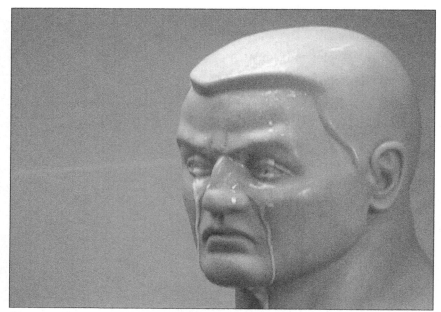

You can develop your pepper spray self-defense skills on the BOB, just be certain to use inert canisters when training.

There's no escaping the fact that mental stress can do a tremendous amount of damage by causing heart disease, high blood pressure, chest pain, and an irregular heartbeat. It's no wonder stress is called the "silent killer."

The good news is; working out on the BOB regularly can be an excellent form of stress reduction. Punching and kicking an inanimate object, such as the body opponent bag, permits you to channel pent-up aggression in a productive fashion.

Cardiovascular Conditioning

If you workout on the body opponent bag with a significant amount of intensity, you can turn it into a cardiovascular workout. However, this will require you to really move around the bag and throw your punches, kicks and strikes at a respectable pace. Keep in mind, if you deliver your

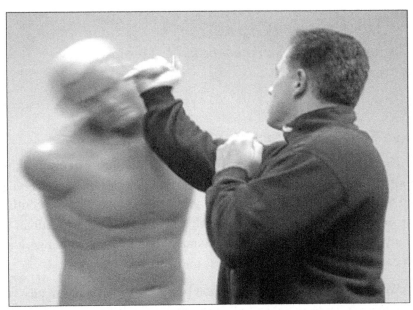

The BOB can also be used for developing your weapon skills. In this photo, the author strikes the body opponent bag with a kubotan mini stick.

blows and strikes with full power and intensity, your workout will quickly become an anaerobic workout and you will most likely fizzle out.

Body opponent bag sessions can last anywhere from 30 seconds to 5 minutes depending on your level of conditioning, personal goals and training objectives.

Improving Muscle Tone

Body opponent bag training can also improve the muscle tone in your entire body including your back, chest, shoulders, arms, chest, abs, legs and calves. A typical workout can also burn a significant amount of calories and therefore can be a good method for stripping fat from the body.

> *"While body opponent bag training does improve muscle tone it should not be used as a substitute for weight training."*

Anger Management Tool

Unless you live on your own island, you will most likely live in a populated region that puts you in contact with many people everyday. Add a hectic lifestyle to the mix and you will most likely have conflicts with other people from time to time. This is when you will sometimes get the urge to respond in a "physical manner" but as a law abiding citizen you can't act on this and must repress these primitive urges.

Working out on the body opponent bag allows you to physically vent toxic anger in an acceptable and appropriate way. It's no wonder the bag is one of the most recommended items for children and adults in therapy.

> *"Punching and kicking an inanimate object, such as a body opponent bag, permits you to channel pent-up aggression in a productive fashion."*

Bob's Only Drawback!

There really is only one real drawback to the body opponent bag and it's his head! As I mentioned earlier, the body opponent bag is ideal for specialized self-defense training like, open hand strikes, weapons training, choking techniques, etc. However, when it comes to throwing powerful head shots, the body opponent bag has limitations.

More specifically, the head of the body opponent bag is light and flexible and cannot withstand the effect of power punching. It simply doesn't offer the resistance necessary for a serious heavy hitter.

That's not to say that you can't develop powerful kicks, punches, and strikes on the BOB. You can! As a matter of fact, the torso of the body opponent bag provides tremendous resistance against powerful body shots and will give the most seasoned fighter a great workout.

If you're determined to throw power punches to BOB's head, you can have your training partner stabilize it while delivering punches.

CHAPTER TWO
Getting Started

Finding The Right Location

One important considerations when setting up the body opponent bag is finding the right location for training. First, you will need a place that will allow you to move around the bag. The location you choose should be a quiet place that is free from distractions. Here are a few locations you might want to consider when setting up your bag:

- Garage
- Carport
- Basement
- Barn
- Home gym (if you are fortunate enough)
- Warehouse
- Under a Deck

One of the greatest benefits of owning a BOB is that you don't have to deal with the daunting issues of installing a heavy bag mounting system. For example, if you owned a traditional heavy bag, you would have to find a beam to hang the bag or install a mount hanger into the wall stud.

"One of the greatest benefits of owning a BOB is that you don't have to deal with the daunting issues of installing a heavy bag mounting system."

If you can manage to clear out the clutter from your garage, it can be a perfect location for body opponent bag training.

Filling Up the Base

Once you find the ideal location for training, the next task is filling the body opponent bag. Essentially, you have one of three options when filling the base. They are:

- Water

- Sand

- Pea gravel

If you plan on using a dry weight material perform the following steps: Unscrew the cap located on the top of the base, insert a funnel into the hole and carefully pour the material into the base. When the base appears full, secure the cap and tilt the base side to side to evenly distribute the material. Continue refilling the material if necessary.

If you are using water to fill the base perform the following. Unscrew the cap, insert a water hose into the hole and fill the base within two inches of the threaded inlet. Replace the cap. **Important:** After using the BOB a few times, unscrew the cap and let any air pressure escape from the base.

Setting the Proper Height

Now it's time to set the proper height of the body opponent bag. This is especially important for people who intend on using the BOB for self-defense or sport combat competition like mixed martial arts. For all practical purposes, the top of the BOB should be approximately head level with you. This will ensure that your targets are realistic.

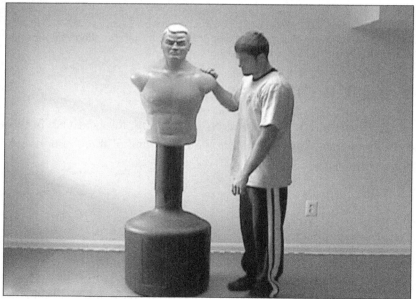

Pictured here, the ideal height for BOB training.

Adjusting the height of the BOB is easy. In fact, the base of the body opponent bag allows you to adjust the height of the mannequin to seven different positions, each one in three-inch increments.

16

The stem of the body opponent bag allows you to adjust the height of the bag to seven different positions, each one in three inch increments.

Begin by placing the torso of the BOB on the stem of the base. This is accomplished by aligning the lock pins (inside the torso) with the channels on the stem. Once properly aligned, the torso should slide effortlessly down the stem and to the base.

To change the hight of the bag, perform the following:

1. Align the lock pins with the stem channel and slide the torso upwards three inches at a time until it reaches the desired height.

2. Next, twist the torso of the mannequin until the lock pins slide to the ends of the channel and fall into place.

BOB Nomenclature

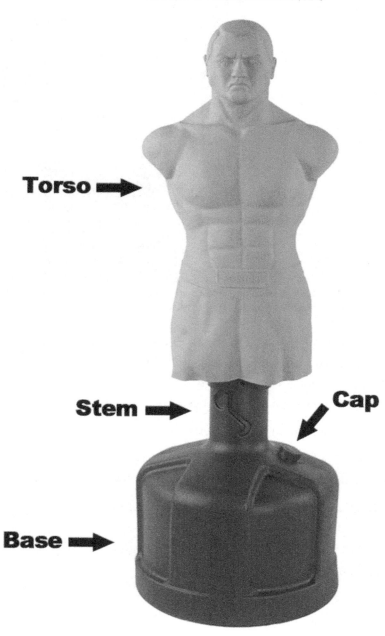

Torso ➡

Stem ➡

Cap

Base ➡

You can adjust the torso of the mannequin to meet your personal workout preference. In this photo, the author prepares to fight a much taller adversary.

Moving the BOB

One of the greatest benefits of the body opponent bag is the ability to transport it quickly and easily. If you plan to move the body opponent bag a short distance, try the rolling technique. To perform this, do the following:

1. Remove the mannequin torso from the stem.

2. Make certain the cap is tight and secure.

3. Grab the top of the stem and carefully tilt the unit to you.

4. While in the tilt position, carefully roll the base to the desired location.

If you plan to relocate the BOB a greater distance, your best bet is to load it on a two-wheeled hand dolly. Important: Never attempt to lift a filled body opponent bag unit.

Body Opponent Bag Safety Tips

Before you launch ahead and start hitting the BOB, it's important to go over some important safety tips.

• Consult with your personal physician before beginning this or any other strenuous exercise program.

• Immediately stop training if you feel pain or discomfort.

• To avoid injuries, always begin your workout with a light round first.

• Never hold your breath when working out on the bag.

• Always remember to exhale when delivering a blow to the bag.

• Always keep your workout area clear of objects.

• While punching or kicking the BOB, make certain that no one is standing near the bag. This includes pets.

• When setting up the BOB always follow the manufacturer's instructions.

• To avoid hyper-extending your arm, never strike the bag unless you are absolutely certain you will make contact.

• Always warm up with light stretching before working out on the bag.

• Never place your BOB directly next to a window.

• Before working out, always check and make certain the torso is securely seated in the stem channel.

- When working out on the body opponent bag, remember to keep both of your hands up always.

- Always wear loose fitting clothing when working out.

- To avoid injuring your hands and damaging your BOB, never workout with rings or jewelry on your hands.

- Never strike the BOB with full-force until you have mastered the proper punching body mechanics.

- To avoid spraining or breaking your wrists, never bend your wrists when punching the bag.

- Don't strike the BOB with bare knuckles until your hands are conditioned to withstand the impact.

- Get into the habit of timing your rounds.

- Proper punching and kicking form is always more important than intensity.

- Never fully extend or "lock out" your arms when punching the bag.

- Depending on the type of punch or kick that you are executing, always maintain the correct distance from the bag.

- Never allow people to play or swing from the BOB.

- Avoid lifting your chin and exposing your centerline when working out on the bag.

- Maintain proper footwork and stay balanced always when working out.

- If your hands are sore from a previous workout, consider wearing a pair of boxing gloves the next time you work out.

Body Opponent Bag Gear

If you want to get the most out of your workouts, you might want to invest in some gear. Here are a few items you might want to consider buying to help you with your training.

Bag Gloves

Bag gloves are lightweight gloves that offer excellent protection to your hands when working out on all types of punching bags.

Bag gloves are constructed of either top grain cowhide or durable vinyl. There are generally two styles of bag gloves that are sold on the market:

- **Mitt style gloves**
- **Finger style gloves**

Some mitt style bag gloves may also have a small mental bar sewn into the palm grip area to aid in fist stabilization. Bag glove sizes are usually small, medium, large and extra large.

Pictured here, mitt style bag gloves.

Pictured here, finger style bag gloves.

When buying bag gloves, spare no expense and look for a reputable and high quality brand. This will provide years of reliable use and will help ensure a better quality workout.

If you don't think you will need bag gloves, think again. Punching the body opponent bag without hand protection causes sore knuckles, bruised bones, hand inflammation, sore wrists and scraped knuckles. What is more important, it will set your training back for several weeks in order for your hands to heal.

Boxing Gloves

People often confuse bag gloves with boxing gloves. While the two might appear similar, they are quite different. Boxing gloves are heavier and significantly larger than bag gloves and they are generally used for full contact sparring sessions and sport combat competition.

However, boxing gloves also can be used for BOB training. In fact, advanced practitioners often use boxing gloves for developing strength and endurance in their arms.

The ideal boxing glove is one that provides comfort, protection, and durability. Depending on your training objectives, the glove can weigh anywhere from ten to sixteen ounces.

In this photo, a standard pair of boxing gloves.

Here are some important features to be aware of when buying a pair of boxing gloves:

- To avoid wrist injuries, you want the glove to fit snugly around your hand.

- The boxing glove should be composed of multilayered foam padding.

- The glove should have a sufficient palm grip that provides comfort and fist stabilization.

- To avoid a thumb injury, the glove should have thumb-lock stitching.

- The glove should be double-stitched to ensure durability.

- The entire glove should be constructed of top quality materials to increase its durability.

- The glove should be easy to slip-on and off your hands. Velcro fasteners are preferred over laces!

As you can see, there's a significant difference between the bag glove (right) and the boxing glove (left).

"When buying bag gloves, spare no expense and look for a reputable and high quality brand. This will provide years of reliable use and will help ensure a better quality workout."

Hand Wraps

Hand Wraps are used by experienced athletes who want an added measure of protection to their hands when hitting the bag. They provide support for the entire hand and wrist area and can help prevent osteoarthritis in later years.

Essentially, hand wraps are long strips of cloth measuring two inches wide and nine to eighteen feet long. Longer hand wraps are used by practitioners who have large hands and who wish to have greater hand protection. You can find hand wraps at most sporting goods stores as well as the internet.

Hand wraps should only be used in conjunction with either large bag gloves or boxing gloves, do not strike the bag with just your hand wraps as this can easily injure your hands.

Hand wraps are washable and should be cleaned after every workout. Although there is a wide range of hand wrapping techniques, the procedures shown on page 29 is suggested.

While hand wraps are a necessary piece of training equipment for boxing, mixed martial arts and other competitive combat sports, I don't recommend using them for self-defense training.

A close-up view of hand wraps.

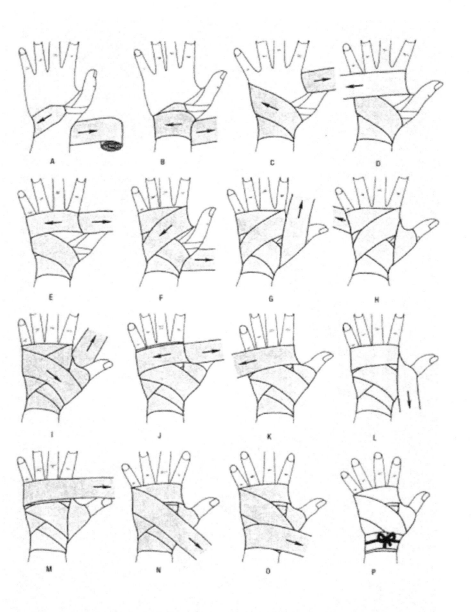

How to wrap your hands with hand wraps. Follow steps A through P.

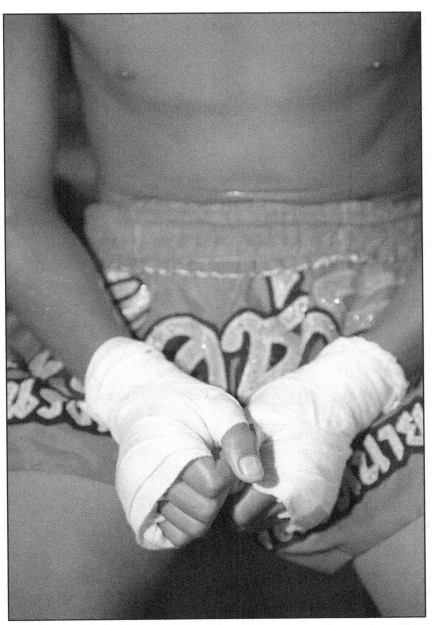

Hand wraps are used all over the world by many cultures. Here, a Muay Thai fighter takes a break during his training.

Interval Workout Timer

Since body opponent bag training is structured around time and rounds, you should invest in a good workout timer. Workout timers are used by boxers, mixed martial artists, kick boxers, and fitness enthusiasts to keep track of their time during their rounds.

Most workout timers will allow you to adjust your round lengths anywhere from thirty seconds to nine minutes. Rest time can be adjusted from thirty seconds to five minutes depending on your level of conditioning and training goals.

There are a wide variety of timers that are sold on the market and they will vary in price. Your best bet is to search the internet for a timer that meets your specific needs.

Workout Timers are great for:

• Keeping track of the number of rounds and the time of each round when working out alone.

• Measuring your current level of cardiovascular conditioning.

• Monitoring your progress in your training.

• Creating healthy competition in your workout routine.

Heart Rate Monitor

Body opponent bag workouts are challenging and can really tax your cardiovascular system. For those of you who would like to track the intensity of your workouts, you might want to consider buying a heart rate monitor.

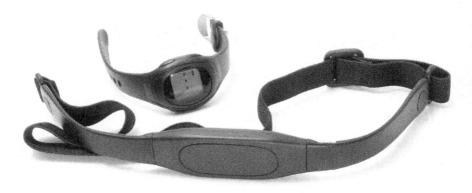

In this photo, a heart rate monitor. To avoid damaging the watch component of the monitor, don't wear it on your wrist when hitting the bag. Instead, consider placing it on a shelf or in your pocket when working out. Keep it close by so you check your heart rate from time to time during your workout.

"*Body opponent bag training can be very demanding on the heart. Before you begin any punching bag workout program, including those suggested in this book, it is important to check with your physician to see whether you have any condition that might be aggravated by strenuous exercise.*"

CHAPTER THREE
Stance and Mobility

The Fighting Stance

Whether you are a boxer, mixed martial artist, street fighter, or fitness junkie, you'll need to learn about the fighting stance.

The fighting stance is a strategic and aggressive posture you assume when squared-off with the body opponent bag and it's the foundation for all your punching, kicking and footwork techniques.

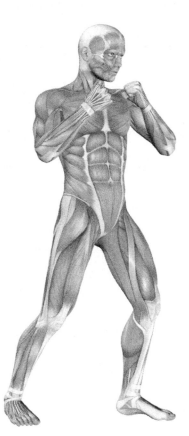

When working out on the body opponent bag, the fighting stance will provide the following:

- Speed

- Power

- Mobility

- Balance and Stability

- Offensive fluidity

- Maximizes limb extension

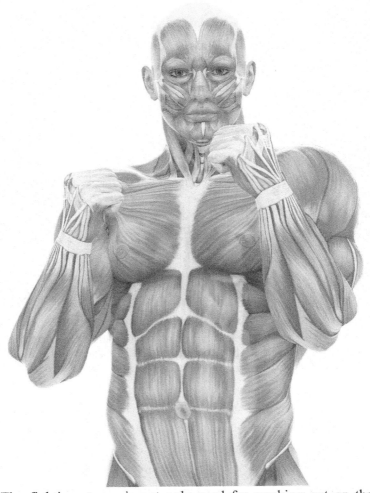

The fighting stance is not only used for working out on the body opponent bag. In actual combat, the fighting stance is used for both offensive and defensive purposes. It stresses strategic soundness and simplicity over complexity and style. The fighting stance also facilitates maximum execution of punches, kicks and strikes while simultaneously protecting your targets against possible counter strikes from the opponent.

The fighting stance is not only used for working out on the BOB. In fact, a good stance sets the foundation for both offensive and defensive techniques. In this photo, the author (left) executes a low line side kick to his assailant's knee.

The key to the fighting stance is the centerline. Your centerline is an imaginary vertical line that divides your body in half. Located on this line are some of your vital targets (eyes, nose, chin, throat, solar plexus, and groin). When working out it's important to position or angle your centerline approximately forty-five degrees from the bag.

"The fighting stance stresses strategic soundness and simplicity over complexity and style."

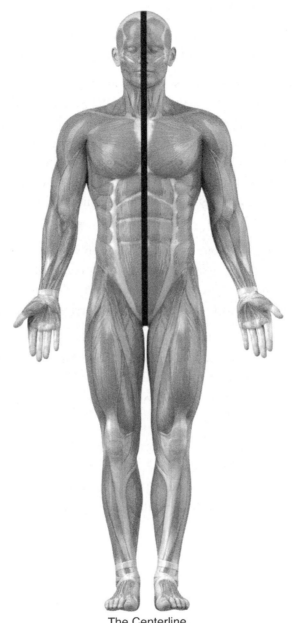

The Centerline.

How To Assume a Fighting Stance

Essentially, there are two variations of the fighting stance, the orthodox and southpaw. Let's begin with the orthodox stance.

To assume the orthodox stance, place the left side of your body forward and closest to the bag. Then, blade your feet and centerline at approximately forty-five degrees from your bag. Make certain to place your feet approximately a shoulder-width apart with both of your knees bent and flexible. When working out on the body opponent bag, your weight will shift constantly; however your weight distribution for the fighting stance should begin with fifty percent of your weight on each leg.

Next, keep both of your hands up and align your lead hand in front of the rear. When holding up your hand guard, make certain not to tighten your shoulders or arms. Stay relaxed and loose. Finally, keep your chin slightly angled down with your eyes looking forward at the bag.

If you want to assume a southpaw fighting stance, you would perform the very same steps mentioned above but with your right side facing forward and closest to the BOB. Generally, most right handed people with use the orthodox stance while left handed people will opt for the southpaw.

However, for those who are interested in reality based self-defense, you must be able to fight your adversary with equal ability on both the right and left sides of your body. This means that you would need to practice bag work from both the southpaw and orthodox stances.

Stay relaxed and loose. Finally, keep your chin slightly angled down with your eyes looking forward at the bag.

The Orthodox Fighting Stance.

The Southpaw Fighting Stance.

One common mistake is to stand squarely in front of the body opponent bag without regard to your stance. Never stand squarely in front of the bag. Not only will this expose your centerline targets, it also diminishes your balance, inhibits efficient footwork, and minimizes your reach. Always try to maintain a forty-five degree angle from the bag.

The classic "boxer's stance" is actually an orthodox fighting stance. Notice how the centerline of his body is angled at approximately 45 degrees.

When assuming a stance, avoid the tendency to let both your elbows flair out to the sides. This type of elbow positioning is bad because it places your hands out of proper body mechanic alignment.

The fighting stance can be used for many different purposes, including reality based self-defense. Here, the author demonstrates a left lead or orthodox fighting stance. Again, notice how the centerline of his body is positioned at approximately forty-five degrees. Also, if you are interested in reality based self-defense training then you will need to become proficient with both the orthodox and southpaw fighting stances.

Mobility

Now, that we have the fighting stance covered, it's time to talk about mobility and footwork. One mistake beginners make when working out on the body opponent bag is to simply stand in front of it and beat it to death! While this methodology might have some street fighting applications, it should not be your sole method of training on the BOB.

Footwork

When working out on the BOB, you must integrate mobility with your punching and kicking techniques. This means that you will need to learn some of the basics of footwork.

The most efficient footwork for body opponent training involves quick economical steps performed on the balls of your feet, while you remain relaxed and balanced. When moving on the balls of your feet, always try to keep your legs a shoulder-width apart and your weight evenly distributed. Moving on the balls of your feet does not mean haphazardly dancing around the bag. This type of "show boating" is pointless and will most likely develop bad habits.

In all forms of unarmed combat, basic footwork can be used for both offensive and defensive purposes, and it is structured around moving in four general directions:

- **Moving forward (advance)** - from your stance, first move your front foot forward (approximately twelve inches) and then move your rear foot an equal distance.

- **Moving backward (retreat)** - from your stance, first move your rear foot backward (approximately twelve inches) and then move your front foot an equal distance.

- **Moving sideways right (sidestep right)** - from your stance, first move your right foot to the right (approximately twelve inches) and then move your left foot an equal distance.

42

- **Moving sideways left (sidestep left)** - from your stance, first move your left foot to the left (approximately twelve inches) and then move your right foot an equal distance.

Circling Around the BOB

Since BOB training will require you to circle around it, you must be aware of advanced footwork that requires you to circle your body around the object. This is known as strategic circling.

Strategic circling is an advanced form of footwork where you will use your front leg as a pivot point. This type of footwork can also be used defensively to evade an overwhelming assault or offensively to strike the opponent from various strategic angles. Strategic circling can be performed from either an orthodox or southpaw stance.

Circling left (from an orthodox stance) - Circling to the left from an orthodox stance means you'll be moving your body around the bag in a clockwise direction.

From an orthodox stance, step eight to twelve inches to the left with your left foot, then use your left leg as a pivot point and wheel your entire rear leg to the left until the correct stance and positioning is acquired.

Circling right (from a southpaw stance) - From a southpaw stance, step eight to twelve inches to the right with your right foot, then use your right leg as a pivot point and wheel your entire rear leg to the right until the correct stance and positioning is acquired.

Avoid Cross-Stepping When Hitting The Bag

Cross-stepping is the process of crossing one foot in front or behind the other when moving around the bag. Such sloppy footwork makes you vulnerable to a variety of problems. Some include:

43

- It severely compromises your balance.

- It restricts the offensive flow of punching.

- It limits quick and rapid footwork.

- It can lead to a sprained ankle.

The best way to avoid cross-stepping is to follow this basic footwork rule of thumb: *Always move the foot closest to the direction you want to go first, and let the other foot follow an equal distance.*

Reality is the key! Try to visualize the bag as a living breathing opponent who will hit back the moment you get your guard down.

"In order for you to maximize your BOB workouts you must integrate mobility with your punching and kicking techniques. Avoid the natural tendency to just stand there and beat the bag to death."

CHAPTER FOUR
How to Punch

Injury Free Punching

Since most of your body opponent bag techniques will be delivered with your fists, it's essential that you know how to punch without sustaining a hand injury. Essentially, this requires you to understand and ultimately master a few concepts and body mechanic principles. Keep in mind that you don't have to be a professional boxer or martial arts expert to master these basic principles.

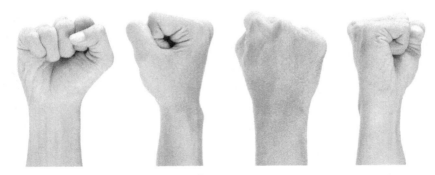

What Causes Hand Injuries?

Essentially, there are four main causes of punching related hand injuries. They are:

- Incorrect fist configuration

- Skeletal misalignment

- Weak hands, wrist, and forearms

- Hitting the wrong target

While there are different body mechanics for each punch, there are four things that must take place to avoid a hand injury when hitting the bag. They include the following:

- Knowing how to make a proper fist.

- Possessing strong hands, wrists, and forearms.

- Maintaining skeletal alignment when your fist reaches the bag.

- Target accuracy.

Making a Proper Fist

The first thing you need to do is learn the proper way make a fist. It's ironic how some of the most experienced fighters and martial artists don't know how to make a proper fist. As you can imagine, improper fist clenching can be disastrous for some of the following reasons:

- You can jam, sprain, or break your fingers.

- You can destroy wrist alignment, resulting in a sprained or broken wrist.

- You'll lose significant power when hitting the bag.

To make a proper fist, make certain that your fingers are tightly clenched and that your thumb is securely wrapped around your second and third knuckles. You fist should look resemble a solid flat brick. Remember to keep in mind, if you can't make a proper fist, you won't be capable of delivering a solid punch on the BOB!

Pictured here, the correct way to make a fist.

"It's actually ironic how some of the most experienced fighters and martial artists don't know how to make a proper fist."

You Must Keep Everything Straight

Now, that you know how to make a proper fist, your next step is learning how to maintaining skeletal alignment when your fist reaches the bag. Skeletal alignment will help ensure that both your hand and wrists won't buckle and break when it hits the bag.

Center Knuckle Contact

To maintain skeletal alignment when punching, you need to learn to punch with your center knuckle first. Punching with the center of your knuckle is important because it affords proper alignment and maximizes the power of your blow.

One of the biggest mistakes beginners make when learning how to make a fist is allowing their thumbs to protrude outward. This type of hand position is dangerous and can often lead to hand and finger injuries as well as powerless blows. Please remember to always keep your thumbs tightly wrapped around the other two fingers when throwing punches.

Excluding hammer fist strikes, every conceivable punch (i.e., jabs, rear cross, hooks, upper cuts, shovel hooks, etc) can be delivered with center knuckle contact.

Center knuckle contact also prevents a broken hand or "boxer's fracture" from occurring. Essentially, a boxer's fracture occurs when the small metacarpal bone bends downward and to the palm of the hand when striking an extremely hard surface (such as a brick wall or human skull).

Contrary to what karate schools teach, I suggest that you avoid striking the body opponent bag with your first two knuckles. This common karate style of punching diffuses the weight transfer of the punch that can easily lead to a broken hand.

"Skeletal alignment will help ensure that both your hand and wrists won't buckle and break during impact with the body opponent bag."

Wrist and Forearm Alignment

If you want to avoid breaking or spraining your wrists you must remember to always keep your wrists aligned with your forearm throughout the execution of your punch. This applies to both linear punches (jab, lead straights, rear cross) as well as circular punches (hooks, uppercuts, and shovel hooks).

If your wrist bends or collapses on impact, you will either sprain or break it. It's that simple. Remember, a sprained or broken wrist will set back your bag training for months.

Don't make the false assumption that boxing gloves or hands wraps will keep your wrists straight. I know of several fighters who sprained their wrists while wearing hand wraps and boxing gloves.

If you want to avoid breaking or spraining your wrists, you must remember to always keep your wrists aligned with your forearm throughout the execution of your punch.

Ironically, one of the best ways to learn how to throw a punch without bending your wrists is to regularly workout on the body opponent bag. The bag will provide the necessary amount of resistance to progressively strengthen and condition the bones, tendons, and ligaments in your wrists. Just remember to start off slowly and progressively increase the force of your punches.

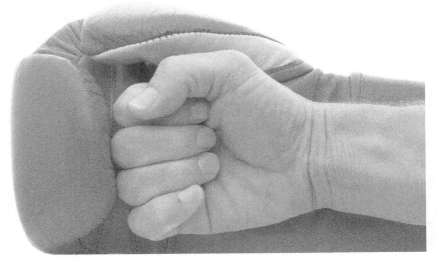

Don't make the false assumption that boxing gloves or bag gloves will keep your wrists straight.

"Ironically, one of the best ways to learn how to throw a punch without bending your wrists is to regularly workout on the body opponent bag."

Strong Hands, Wrists and Forearms

Proper fist configuration and wrist alignment are important, but that's really only half of the equation. You must have strong hands, wrists, and forearms to withstand the actual force of hitting the body opponent bag.

You will, therefore, need to perform specific exercises to strengthen the muscles of the hands, wrists and forearms.

Bruce Lee was well aware of this important fact. As a matter of fact, he would religiously strengthen and develop his hands and forearms for the rigors of power punching.

Lee knew that powerful and injury free punching depends largely on the overall strength and structural integrity of your hands, wrists, and forearms. As a result, he would often perform wrist curls, reverse curls and gripping exercises.

The late Bruce Lee knew a thing or two about forearm conditioning for punching proficiency.

"You must have strong hands, wrists, and forearms to withstand the actual force of hitting the body opponent bag."

Training Your Arms and Hands for BOB Training

There are many efficient ways of strengthening your hands, wrists, and forearms for bag training. If you are low on cash and just starting, you can begin by squeezing a tennis ball a couple times per week. One hundred repetitions per hand would be a good start.

Later on you can add power putty to your strengthening routine. This unique hand exerciser is made up of silicone rubber that can be squeezed, pulled, pinched, clawed, and stretched in any conceivable direction. This tough resistant putty will strengthen the muscles of your forearm, wrists, hands, and fingers.

Another quick and effective way to strengthen your hands, wrists and forearms are to work out with heavy-duty hand grippers. While there is a wide selection of them on the market, I prefer using the Captains of Crush brand. These high quality grippers are virtually indestructible, and they come in a variety of different resistance levels ranging from 60 to 365 pounds.

Finally, you can also condition your wrists and forearms by performing various forearm exercises with free weights.

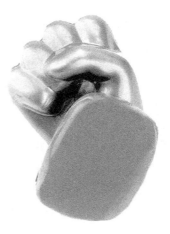

Pictured here, power putty.

Captains of Crush hand grippers are the best on the market!

Accuracy Counts!

The final component of injury free punching is target accuracy. For example, in a street fight you must avoid hitting hard body surfaces like the opponent's skull.

Believe it or not, many self-defense hand injuries are a result of striking the opponent's skull! The human skull is extremely hard and resilient. It's likened to an armor helmet that protects the human brain from impact. I know several fighters who broke their hands when their fists connected with an opponent's forehead or skull.

When it comes to body opponent bag training, you too must be careful where you place your punches. It's important that your strikes are accurate and your punches are timed correctly. This can be especially challenging considering that the BOB can move in unpredictable directions. Just keep in mind that one misplaced power punch can easily sprain or break your wrist.

Be Aware of What You Are Doing!

Learning how to punch correctly also means you will have to study and observe every punch in your arsenal and make certain they can handle the rigors of bag work. Through proper analytical observation, you can quickly identify the strengths and weaknesses of each punch in your arsenal. The best way to accomplish this is to test each punch on the body opponent bag.

For example, lets take the most basic punch known to man - the rear cross. For those who may not be aware, the rear cross is one of the most powerful punches in a fighter's arsenal.

Begin by standing approximately four to five feet from the bag. Then, assume a fighting stance with your left leg forward and your body positioned at a forty-five degree angle from the bag. Make certain both of your hands are properly clenched into fists and your head and chin are angled slightly down.

Now, deliver the punch, exhale and quickly twist and throw your rear arm and shoulder forward and to the bag. Make certain to twist your rear

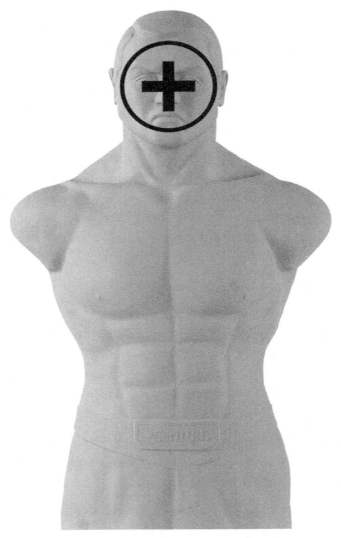

Unlike the heavy bag, the body opponent bag is designed to improve the accuracy of your striking techniques.

leg, hip, and shoulder forward and extend your rear arm ⸱
lock out your rear arm when throwing the punch, be certa
is slightly bent. Your punch should forcefully snap into the l ⸗ and then
return to the starting position. For more information about the rear cross,
see Chapter 5.

After delivering the punch to the bag, make the following important observations:

- What was the overall feeling of the punch when you delivered it? Did it feel rigid and forced or was it loose and fluid?

- What happened when your punch connected with the bag? Did the punch snap or crack the bag? Or did it just nudge it?

- Did anything feel strained or hurt when your fist initially connected with the bag?

- Was your punch accurate? Did you hit the bag exactly where you intended?

- Did you remember to exhale or did you hold your breath when you threw the punch?

- What happened to the structural integrity of your fist when it hit the punching bag? Did your fists open? Did your thumb get in the way? Did your wrist buckle inward?

- Which knuckle made initial contact with the punching bag?

You also might want to consider video taping yourself so you can quickly identify mistakes and errors in your punching form. Or you can have your training partner observe your punching technique and give you constructive feedback.

"Learning how to punch correctly also means you will have to study and observe each punch in your arsenal, and making certain they can handle the rigors of body opponent bag work."

If you really want to see your skills and abilities, video tape your BOB sessions. The video will provide you with a more accurate picture of what you are doing in your training. You will be able to observe punching errors and recognize your strengths and weaknesses. The video recorder will also motivate you to train harder. Save the video tapes and mark the date on each one. Later on you will be able to make comparisons and see marked improvements in your performance.

Punching Mitts

If you find the body opponent bag to be a bit awkward, you can always start off with the punching mitts (also called focus mitts) to examine your punching form.

Unlike the body opponent bag, the punching mitts are more forgiving on your wrists and hands and will allow you to progressively build up your power as your punching form improves.

Punching mitts will challenge even the most seasoned fighter by improving both offensive and defensive fighting skills, punching speed, stamina, rhythm, endurance, accuracy, timing, reflexes, footwork, punching combinations, punching power and counter punching techniques.

The only downside to working with the punching mitts is they will require a training partner to hold them for you. The good news is, once you have learned how to punch on the mitts you can then graduate to the

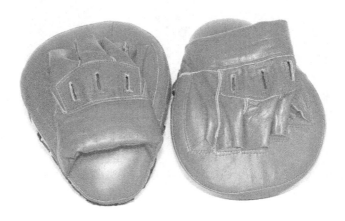

Unlike the body opponent bag, the punching mitts are more forgiving on your wrists and hands and will allow you to progressively build up your power as your punching form improves.

body opponent bag where you can test delivering your punches with full force.

"If you find the body opponent bag to be a bit awkward to work with, you can always start off with the punching mitts to examine your punching form."

CHAPTER FIVE
Targets & Techniques

BOB Targets

One of the biggest mistakes you can make when working out on the body opponent bag, is to strictly hit the mannequin head on. Since BOB's anatomically targets are located on all sides of the bag, you should take full advantage and move around it when training. Let's take a look at some of BOB's targets.

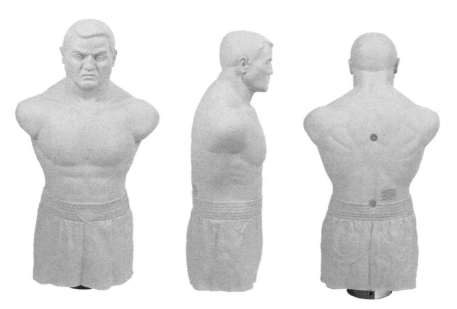

Anatomical targets are located all around the body opponent bag, so remember to move around it when working out.

Front ViewTargets

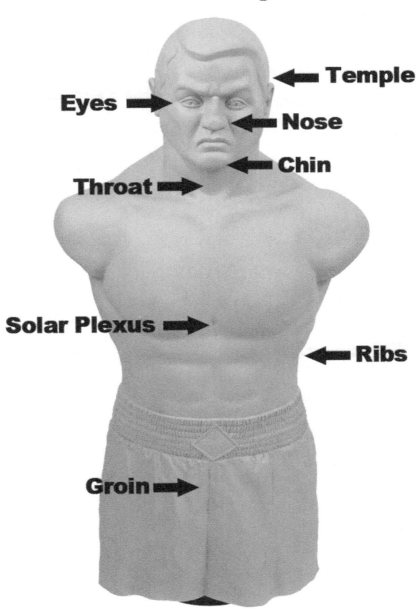

Temple

Eyes

Nose

Chin

Throat

Solar Plexus

Ribs

Groin

Side View Targets

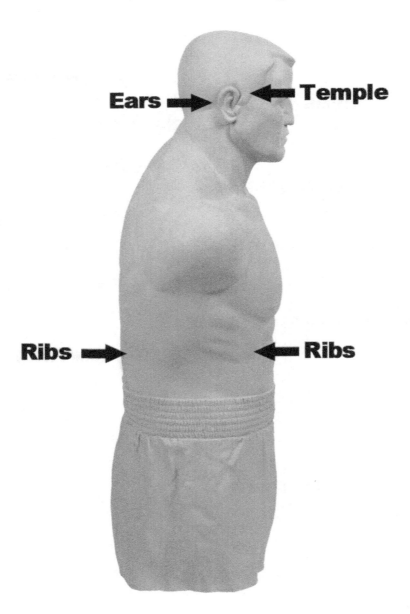

Ears ➡   ⬅ Temple

Ribs ➡   ⬅ Ribs

Rear View Targets

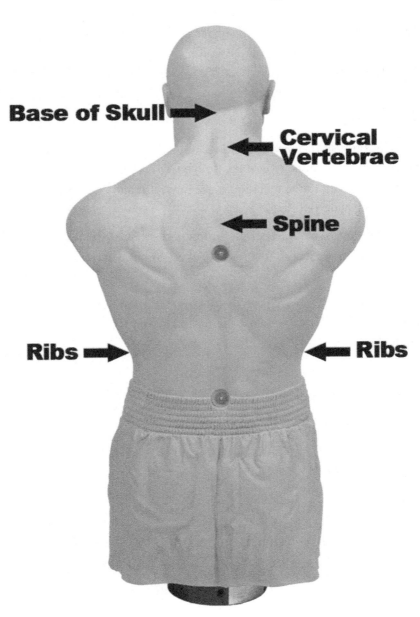

Base of Skull

Cervical Vertebrae

Spine

Ribs

Ribs

Combat Ranges

Now, before we get into specific body opponent bag techniques, you first need to understand that the distance and angle of the BOB will often dictate which striking technique you can execute at any given moment. Therefore, you must know about the three combat ranges. They include: kicking, punching, and grappling range. Let's begin with kicking range.

Kicking Range

The furthest distance is kicking range. At this range you are usually too far away to punch the bag, so you would use your legs to make contact. Kicking range techniques are powerful and can give your legs a tremendous workout.

Important: If you are strictly interested in BOB training for boxing, you can skip this and focus exclusively on the next section of this chapter.

While there is a myriad of kicking techniques in the martial arts world, here's a list of some of the basic kicking techniques you can use on the bag:

- Push kick (front leg)
- Push kick (back leg)
- Side kick (front leg)
- Hook kick (front leg)
- Hook kick (back leg)

"You first need to understand that the distance and angle of the BOB will often dictate which striking technique you can execute at any given moment."

In this photo, the kicking range of unarmed combat.

Push Kick (from the front leg)

1. To perform the kick, begin from an orthodox stance (left side forward).

2. While maintaining your balance, shift your weight onto your back leg and raise your front leg up (your front knee should be bent at approximately 90 degrees).

3. Next, thrust with your hips and drive the ball of your front foot into the bag.

4. After contact is made with the bag, quickly retract your leg to the starting position. Remember to always keep your hands up when performing kicking techniques.

When performing the push kick be certain to hit with the ball of your foot and not your toes. Striking the bag with your toes can easily lead to a severe injury.

Push Kick (from the rear leg)

1. To perform the kick, begin from an orthodox stance (left side forward).

2. While maintaining your balance, push your back foot off the ground and shift your weight to your front leg (your rear knee should be bent at approximately 90 degrees).

3. Next, thrust with your hips and drive the ball of your foot into the bag.

4. After contact is made with the bag, quickly retract your leg to the starting position. Again, make certain to make contact with the ball of your foot and not your toes.

Side Kick (from the front leg)

1. To perform the side kick, begin from an orthodox stance (left side facing the bag).

2. While maintaining your balance, lean back and shift your weight onto your rear leg while simultaneously pivoting your body so your centerline is approximately 90 degrees from the bag.

3. Raise your front knee up and close to your body (this is called the "chamber" position).

4. Next, use your hips and thrust your front leg forcefully into the bag. Contact is made with the heel of your foot.

5. After contact is made with the bag, retract your leg to the starting position.

"When performing kicking techniques, always remember to exhale as you execute the movement."

Hook kick (front leg)

1. To perform the hook kick from your front leg, begin from an orthodox stance (left side facing the bag).

2. While maintaining your balance, lean back slightly and shift your weight to your rear leg.

3. Simultaneously raise your front knee up and towards the bag.

4. Next, quickly twist your front hip and swing your lead leg forcefully into the bag. Your front knee should be slightly bent when contact is made with the target. Avoid snapping your knee when performing the kick. Contact should be made with either the dorsum of your foot or shin bone.

5. After contact is made with the bag, bring your leg back to the starting position.

Hook kick (rear leg)

1. To perform the hook kick from your rear leg, begin from an orthodox stance (left side facing the bag).

2. While maintaining your balance, push off the back foot and shift your weight forward.

3. Next, raise your rear knee up and twist your hips forward as you swing your rear leg forcefully into the bag.

4. Your rear knee should be slightly bent when impact is made with the bag. Avoid snapping your knee when performing the hook kick. Again, contact should be made with either the dorsum of your foot or shin bone.

69

5. After contact is made with the bag, bring your leg back to the starting position.

"The hook kick is also a devastating self-defense technique that can collapse and temporarily immobilize the assailant's leg. Keep in mind that if you strike the assailant's knee you can cause permanent damage to the cartilage, ligaments, tendons, and bones."

Punching Range

The next distance of unarmed combat is punching range and it's the mid-range of fighting. At this distance, you are close enough to the bag to strike it with your fists. Punching range techniques should be quick, efficient and they should be the foundation of your body opponent bag arsenal.

For those of you who are interested in reality based self-defense training, I strongly encourage you to specialize in the punching range. Here are just a few reasons why:

• The opponent's defensive reaction time is reduced in punching range.

• Unlike kicking techniques, you can efficiently neutralize your adversary with punches and other hand strikes.

• Compared to the other ranges of unarmed combat, punching range techniques are more efficient - there is less energy expenditure.

• Punching range techniques are less telegraphic than kicking range tools.

• Compared to grappling range (vertical & horizontal planes), punching range only requires moderate bodily commitment.

• Unlike kicking range, there is less "space requirement" necessary to deploy most of your punching range techniques.

• Unlike grappling range combat, there is no bodily entanglement, so multiple assailants can be fought in the punching range of unarmed combat.

In this photo, the author squares off with the BOB at punching range.

Punching Range Techniques and Western Boxing

Interestingly enough, amateur and professional boxers focus exclusively on the punching range of unarmed combat. Here's a brief list of punching techniques that you can perform on the bag.

- Jab
- Rear cross
- Hook punch
- Uppercut punch

Very little has changed since the golden age of boxing. Amateur and professional boxers alike focus exclusively on punching techniques for their sport.

The Jab

The jab is a foundation technique for boxers and mixed martial artists. This punch is thrown from your front hand, and it has a quick snap when delivered.

1. Start off in a fighting stance with both of your hands held up in the guard position. Your fists should be lightly clenched with both of your elbows pointing to the ground.

2. To perform the punch, simultaneously step to the bag and twist your front waist and shoulder forward as you snap your front arm into the bag.

3. When delivering the punch, remember not to lock out your arm as this will have a "pushing effect" on the bag.

4. Quickly retract your arm back to the starting position.

One common mistake when throwing the jab is to let it deflect off to the side of the bag. Also, keep in mind that jabs can be delivered to the head (top of the bag) or the body (middle of the bag).

"When executing linear punches (i.e. jabs, rear crosses) on the BOB, remember that your line of initiation should always be your line of retraction. Avoid arcing or dropping your blow after contact is made with the bag. Such sloppy body mechanics will throw you off balance and diminish your impact power."

In boxing and mixed martial arts, the jab is an essential punch used to throw the opponent off balance, set him up for other blows, test his reflexes and keep him from moving toward you.

The lead straight is a linear punch thrown from your lead arm and contact is made with the center knuckle. To execute the lead straight, quickly twist your lead leg, hip, and shoulder forward. Snap your blow into the bag and return to the starting position. A common mistake is to throw the punch and let it deflect off to the side of BOB's head.

Using the Jab for Self-Defense

While the jab might be suitable for boxing, mixed martial arts and other forms of combat sport competition, it has no purpose in real world combat. The jab is combatively deficient for some of the following reasons:

- It lacks neutralizing power.

- It can expose you to a counter attack.

- It often agitates the assailant more than it harms him.

- It prolongs a self-defense altercation and allows the assailant the opportunity to escalate his level of force against you.

- It's a probing and point scoring tool.

If self-defense is your interest and concern, you can simply replace the Jab with the Lead Straight punch. Like the jab, the lead straight is also a linear punch thrown from your lead arm; however this punch is more powerful and can be used on the bag as well as real life self-defense situations.

The Jab is the "bread and butter" of any boxing program and it's used in numerous combinations with other punches.

Rear Cross

The rear cross is considered the heavy artillery of punches, and it's thrown from your rear arm. To execute the punch, perform the following steps:

1. Start off in a fighting stance with both of your hands held up in the guard position. Your fists should be lightly clenched with both of your elbows pointing to the ground.

2. To perform the punch, quickly twist your rear hips and shoulders forward as you snap your rear arm into the bag. Proper waist twisting and weight transfer is critical for the rear cross. You must shift your weight from your rear foot to your lead leg as you throw the punch.

3. To maximize the power of the punch, make certain that your fist is positioned horizontally. Avoid overextending the blow or exposing your chin during its execution.

4. Again, do not lock out your arm when throwing the punch. Let the power of the punch sink into the bag before you retract it back to the starting position.

When throwing liner punches, be certain not to lock your elbow. Elbow locking is a common problem among novices. There should always be a slight bend in your elbow when the punch hits the bag. Remember, if your elbow locks on impact, it will have a "pushing effect" and rob you of critical power.

Another common mistake when throwing the rear cross on the body opponent bag is to let the punch glide downwards after contact is made. Always remember, the trajectory of initiating your punch must also be the very same trajectory of retracting your punch.

The rear cross is an extremely powerful punch that can be delivered to both high and low targets on the body opponent bag.

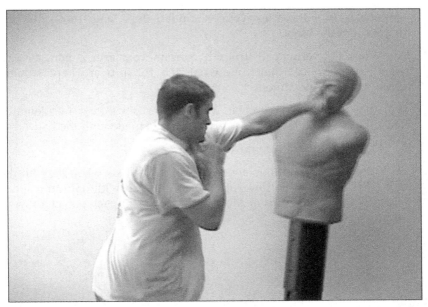

When delivering the rear cross, remember to turn your palm down so your fists hit the bag horizontally.

Hook Punch

The hook is another devastating punch in your arsenal of techniques, yet it's also one of the most difficult to master. This punch can be performed from your front or rear hand and it can be thrown high or low to the bag. There are two variations of the hook punch, they include:

- Traditional Hook Punch

- Modified Hook Punch

However, for the purpose of this book, I will teach you the traditional hook punch that is used in most boxing circles.

1. Start in a fighting stance with your hand guard held up. Both of your elbows should be pointing to the ground, and your fists should be loosely clenched.

2. To execute the hook punch, quickly and smoothly, raise your elbow up so that your arm is parallel to the ground while

simultaneously torquing your shoulder, hip, and foot into the direction of the blow.

3.   When delivering the strike, be certain your arm is bent at least ninety degrees and that your wrist and forearm are kept straight throughout the movement.

4.   As you throw the punch, your fist is positioned horizontally. The elbow should be locked when contact is made with the bag.

5.   Return to the starting position.

6.   Remember to simultaneously tighten your fists when they hit the bag. This action will allow your punch to travel with optimum speed and efficiency, and it will also augment the impact power of your strike.

In this photo, the author delivers a lead hook punch to BOB's ribs.

"The hook punch is one of the most devastating blows in your arsenal. However, it's also one of the most difficult to master. To properly execute the hook punch, you must maintain the proper wrist, forearm, and shoulder alignment."

Pictured here, a hook punch delivered in real-time speed.

Uppercut Punch

The uppercut is another powerful punch that can be delivered from both the lead and rear arm.

1.   Start off in a fighting stance with both of your hands held up in the guard position. Your fists should be lightly clenched with both of your elbows pointing to the ground.

2.   To execute the uppercut, drop your shoulder, and bend your knees.

3.   Quickly, stand up and drive your fist upward and into the bag. Your palm should be facing you when contact is made with the bag. To avoid any possible injury, keep your wrists straight.

4.   Make certain that the punch has a tight arc and that you avoid all "winding up" motions. A properly executed uppercut should be a tight punch and should feel like an explosive jolt.

5.   Return to the fighting stance.

"The real key to delivering a powerful uppercut punch is the lifting of your legs into the direction of your blow."

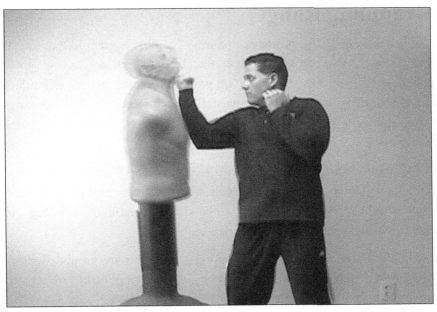

The body opponent bag is great for working the upper cut punch. Pictured here, the author delivers a lead uppercut to the chin.

When performing the uppercut, avoid all wind up motions. Pictured here is what you should <u>not</u> do!

Grappling Range

The third and closest range of unarmed combat is grappling range. At this distance, you are too close to the bag to kick or execute linear punches (i.e., jab, rear cross) so you would use close-quarter techniques to fight your opponent. Several martial art styles specialize in this range of unarmed combat including Jiu-Jitsu, Judo, Russian Sambo and Catch Wrestling.

Grappling range is divided into two different planes; vertical and horizontal. In the vertical plane, you would deliver impact techniques, some of which include elbow and knee strikes, head butts, gouging and crushing tactics, and biting and tearing techniques.

In the horizontal plane of grappling range, you are ground fighting with your opponent and can deliver all the previously mentioned techniques, including various submission holds, locks and chokes.

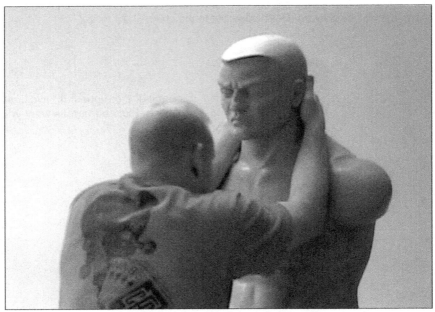

Pictured here, the grappling range.

When it comes to body opponent bag training, grappling range striking techniques are going to appeal to three groups of people:

- Self-defense practitioners
- Mixed martial artists (MMA)
- Martial artists (traditional and eclectics)

You can add several grappling range techniques to your body opponent bag workout. Here are a few:

- Head butts
- Eye rakes
- Elbow strikes
- Neck Cranks
- Knee strikes

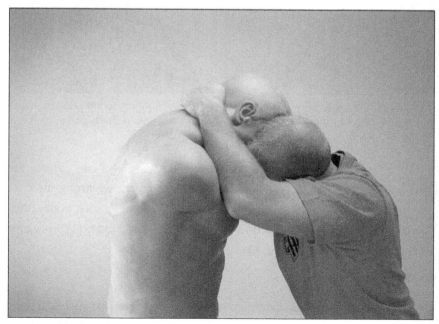

The head butt delivered to the body opponent bag.

Head Butt

The head butt is a very effective close-quarter fighting technique. In this photo, Sammy Franco demonstrates a ramming head butt strike to his assailant's chin.

When squared off with the body opponent bag, you can deliver the head butt strike to his face. Head butts are ideal when a strong attacker has placed you in a hold where your arms are pinned against your sides. The head butt can be delivered in four different directions: (1) Forward; (2) Backward; (3) Right Side; (4) Left Side.

Horizontal Elbow

The elbows are devastating weapons that can be used in the grappling range. They are explosive, deceptive and very difficult to stop.

88

Elbows can generally be delivered horizontally, vertically, diagonally and they can be thrown from either your front or rear arm.

Let's just take a look at the body mechanics of the horizontal elbow strike.

1. Start off in a fighting stance with both of your hands held up in the guard position. Make certain that you are standing in proximity to the bag.

2. To execute the elbow strike, quickly and smoothly, raise your elbow up so that your arm is parallel to the ground.

3. Next, simultaneously torquing your shoulder, hip, and foot into the direction of the bag. The tip of your elbow should reach the target.

4. Return to the starting position.

Pictured here, the lead horizontal elbow delivered to BOB's solar plexus.

Pictured here, a horizontal elbow strike delivered from the rear arm.

You can practice a wide variety of grappling and ground fighting skills on the body opponent bag. In this photo, the author perform the ground and pound technique from grappling range in the vertical plane.

Diagonal Knee Strike

The knee strike is another devastating close-quarter grappling range tool that can do a lot of damage. The knee strike can also be delivered diagonally or vertically to the bag.

Here are the body mechanics of the diagonal knee strike.

- To perform the diagonal knee strike from your rear leg, begin from an orthodox stance (left side facing the bag).

- Next, grab hold of the bag with both hands.

- While maintaining your balance, push off the back foot and shift your weight forward.

- Next, raise your rear knee up and swing your hips and rear leg diagonally into the bag.

- Your rear knee should be sharply bent when it hits the bag.

- After contact is made, bring your leg back to the starting position.

"When delivering knee strikes, keep your rear leg bent with your toe pointed to the ground. This toe position helps maintain proper skeletal alignment; protects your toes from unnecessary injury; and facilitates quick and rapid delivery."

The diagonal knee strike.

Vertical Knee Strike

1. To perform the vertical knee strike from your rear leg, begin from an orthodox stance (left side facing the bag).

2. Next, grab hold of the bag with both hands.

3. While maintaining your balance, push off the back foot and shift your weight forward.

4. Next, raise your rear knee up and drive your hips and rear leg vertically into the bag.

5. Your rear knee should be sharply bent when impact is made with the bag.

6. After contact is made with the bag, bring your leg back to the starting position.

"Grappling Range self-defense techniques include: head butts, biting, tearing, clawing, crushing, gouging, foot stomps, horizontal, vertical, and diagonal elbow strikes, vertical and diagonal knee strikes, chokes, joint locks, holds, reversals and escapes."

CHAPTER SIX
Time Based Workouts

Three Training Methodologies

In this book, I'll provide you with three unique training methodologies that can be applied to body opponent bag training. They include Proficiency Training, Conditioning Training, and Street Training. Let's take a look at each one.

Conditioning Training

Conditioning Training is primarily used by boxers, mixed martial artists, kick boxers, self-defense technicians, and fitness enthusiasts who wish to train on the bag for specified period of time called "rounds". Depending on the practitioner's level of conditioning, each round can range anywhere from one to five minutes. Each round is then separated by either 30-second, one-minute, or two-minute breaks. A good body opponent bag workout consists of at least five to eight rounds.

Conditioning Training is performed at a moderate pace and it develops cardiovascular fitness, muscular endurance, fluidity, rhythm, distancing, timing, speed, footwork, and balance. Many fitness enthusiasts looking to burn fat will use this methodology as it tends to burn a significant amount of calories.

Conditioning Training requires a basic understanding of piecing punches and kicks together into logical combinations.

Proficiency Training

The second training methodology is Proficiency Training and it's generally used by martial artists and self-defense practitioners who want to sharpen one specific punch, kick, or strike at a time by executing it over and over for a prescribed number of repetitions.

Each time the technique is executed with "clean" form at various speeds. Punches are also performed with the eyes closed to develop a kinesthetic "feel" for the action.

96

Proficiency Training on the BOB develops speed, power, accuracy, non-telegraphic movement, balance, and general psychomotor skill.

Street Training

The third and final training methodology is Street Training and it's specifically designed for reality based self-defense preparation.

Since most self-defense altercations are explosive, lasting an average of 20 seconds, the practitioner must prepare for this possible scenario. This means delivering explosive and powerful compound attacks with vicious intent for approximately 20 seconds, resting one minute, and then repeating the process.

Street Training prepares you for the stress and immediate fatigue of a real fight. It also develops speed, power, explosiveness, target selection and recognition, timing, footwork, and breath control.

Designing Your Workout

While all three training methodologies are important, we will focus exclusively on Conditioning Training, which means we are going to use "time based" workouts.

Time Based Workouts

Essentially, a time based body opponent bag workout is based on "rounds" and it's an ideal way to structure your workouts. Before you begin, now is the time to pick the duration of your rounds as well as the rest intervals.

Generally, mixed martial artists, boxers, and kick boxers will work the bag for three minute rounds with one minute rest periods. Depending on their level of conditioning and specific training goals, they might do this for a total of five to eight rounds.

Initially, you'll need to experiment with both the round duration and rest intervals to see what works best for you. Remember to start off slow and progressively build up the intensity and duration of your workouts. Remember to work with the bag and not try to kill it!

To get you started, here are some sample time based workouts you might want to try. Keep in mind, the Advanced Level workouts are for elite fighters who have a minimum of five years of BOB training and conditioning.

Sample Time Based BOB Workouts			
Skill Level	Duration of Each Round	Rest Period	Total Number of rounds
Beginner	1 minute	2 minutes	3
Beginner	1 minute	1 minute	3
Beginner	2 minutes	2 minute	3
Beginner	2 minutes	1 minute	3
Intermediate	3 minutes	2 minutes	5
Intermediate	3 minutes	1 minute	5
Intermediate	3 minutes	2 minute	6
Intermediate	3 minutes	1 minute	6
Advanced	4 minutes	2 minutes	8
Advanced	4 minutes	1 minute	8
Advanced	5 minutes	2 minutes	10
Advanced	5 minutes	1 minute	10

A Word of Caution!

Take your time when working out on the bag. If you are learning how to use the body opponent bag for the very first time, I strongly urge you to take your time and develop the proper punching and kicking body mechanics before tearing into the bag.

Remember, the BOB is a serious piece of training equipment and it's easy to get injured when using it. BOB workouts are also tough and very demanding. Avoid premature exhaustion by pacing yourself during your workouts. Remember, it's not a race! Enjoy the process of learning how to use the bag with skill and finesse.

Warning! Before you begin any exercise program, including those suggested in this book, it is important to check with your physician to see whether you have any condition that might be aggravated by strenuous exercise.

Warming-Up & Stretching Out

Before working out on the body opponent bag, it's important that you first warm up and stretch out. Warming up slowly increases the internal temperature of your body while stretching improves your workout performance, keeps you flexible, and helps reduce the possibility of an injury.

Some of the best exercises for warming up are jumping jacks, rope skipping or a short jog before training. Another effective method of warming up your muscles is to perform light and easy movements with the weights.

When stretching out, keep in mind that all movements should be performed in a slow and controlled manner. Try to hold your stretch for a minimum of sixty seconds and avoid all bouncing movements. You should feel mild tension on the muscle that is being stretched. Remember to stay relaxed and focus on what you are doing. Here are seven stretches that should be performed.

Neck stretch - from a comfortable standing position, slowly tilt your head to the right side of your neck, holding it for a count of twenty. Then tilt your head to the left side for approximately twenty seconds. Stretch each side of the neck at least three times.

100

Triceps stretch - from a standing position, keep your knees slightly bent, extend your right arm overhead, hold the elbow of your right arm with your left hand, and slowly pull your right elbow to the left. Keep your hips straight as you stretch your triceps gently for thirty seconds. Repeat this stretch for the other arm.

Hamstring stretch - from a seated position on the floor, extend your right leg in front of you with your toe pointing to the ceiling. Place the sole of your left foot in the inside of your extended leg. Gently lean forward at the hips and stretch out the hamstrings of your right leg. Hold this position for a minimum of sixty seconds. Switch legs and repeat the stretch.

Spinal twist - from a seated position on the floor, extend your right leg in front of you. Raise your left leg and place it to the outside of your right leg. Place your right elbow on the outside of your left thigh. Stabilize your stretch with your elbow and twist your upper body and head to your left side. Breathe naturally and hold this stretch for a minimum of thirty seconds. Switch legs and repeat this stretch for the other side.

Quad stretch - assume a sitting position on the floor with your hamstrings folded and resting on top of your calves. Your toes should be pointed behind you, and your instep should be flush with the ground. Sit comfortably into the stretch and hold for a minimum of sixty seconds.

Prone stretch - lay on the ground with your back to the floor. Exhale as you straighten your arms and legs. Your fingers and toes should be stretching in opposite directions. Hold this stretch for thirty seconds.

Groin stretch - sit on the ground with the soles of your feet touching each other. Grab hold of your feet and slowly pull yourself forward until mild tension is felt in your groin region. Hold this position for a minimum of sixty seconds.

Now, that you are warmed up and ready to go, here is a weight training program requiring you to train each muscle group two times per week.

"Warning: Before you begin any exercise program, including those suggested in this book, it is important to check with your physician to see whether you have any condition that might be aggravated by strenuous exercise."

Body Opponent Bag Combinations

What is a Combination?

A combination or "compound attack" is the logical sequence of two or more techniques thrown in strategic succession. For example, a jab followed immediately by a rear cross is considered to be a punching combination.

There is an infinite amount of fighting combinations you can perform on the body opponent bag. Frankly, you are only limited by your own creative imagination.

When reading the combination sequence, please note that the word "high" indicates punches delivered at head level on the BOB and the word "low" indicates punches delivered at the stomach level on the bag.

Sample Punching Combinations

What follows are a few punching combinations you can employ in your time based workouts:

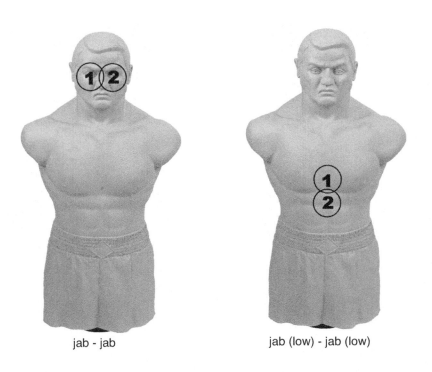

jab - jab   jab (low) - jab (low)

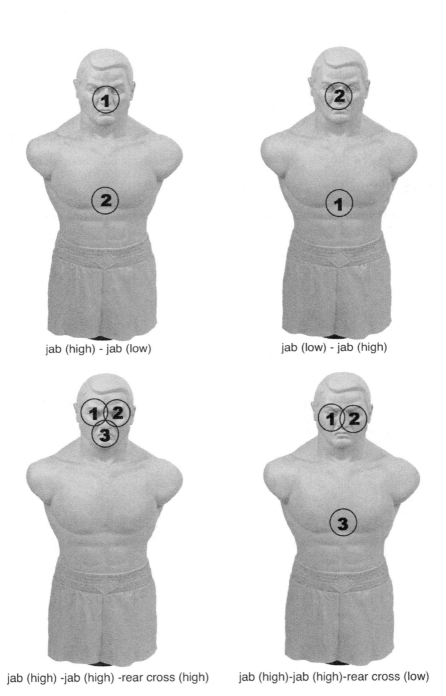

jab (high) - jab (low)

jab (low) - jab (high)

jab (high) -jab (high) -rear cross (high)

jab (high)-jab (high)-rear cross (low)

jab (high) - rear cross (high)

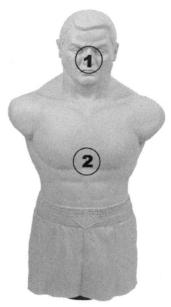

jab (high) - rear cross (low)

jab (high) -rear cross(high) -jab (high)

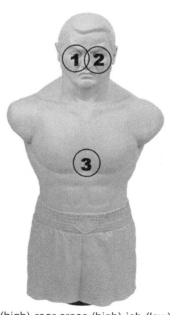

jab (high)-rear cross (high)-jab (low)

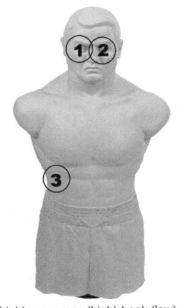

jab (high)-rear cross (low)-hook (high)   jab (high)-rear cross (high)-hook (low)

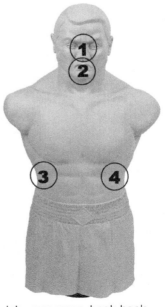

jab -rear cross -hook-hook   jab -rear cross -hook-hook

106

rear cross - hook- hook

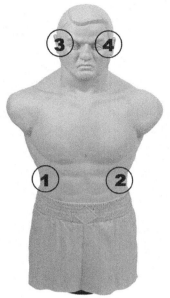

hook - hook- hook- hook

hook - hook- hook- hook

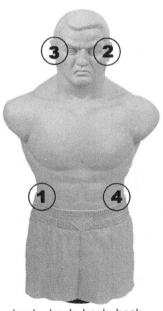

hook - hook- hook- hook

107

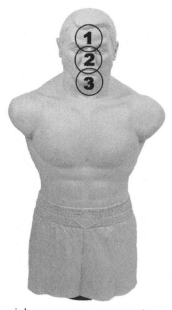

jab -rear cross -uppercut

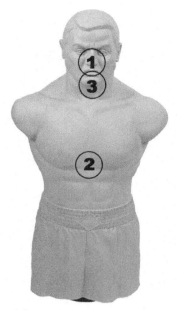

jab -rear cross- uppercut

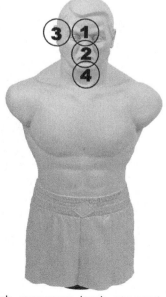

jab -rear cross -hook -uppercut

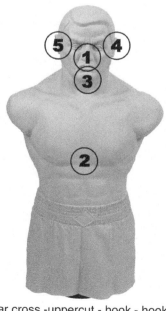

jab -rear cross -uppercut - hook - hook

108

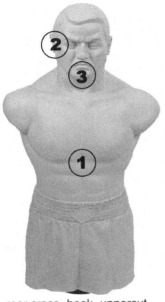

rear cross -hook- uppercut

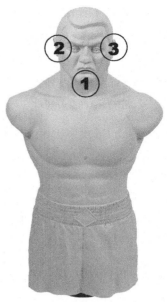

uppercut - hook - hook

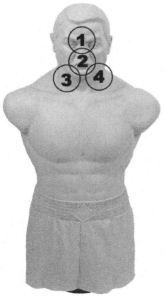

jab -rear cross -uppercut -uppercut

uppercut -uppercut - hook -hook

Punching Combinations

What follows is a complete list of combinations that can be performed on the body opponent bag.

- Jab (high) - Jab (high)
- Jab (low) - Jab (low)
- Jab (high) - Jab (low)
- Jab (low) - Jab (high)
- Jab (high) - Jab (high) - Rear Cross (high)
- Jab (high) - Jab (high) - Rear Cross (low)
- Jab (high) - Rear Cross (high)
- Jab (high) - Rear Cross (low)
- Jab (high) - Rear Cross (high) - Jab (high)
- Jab (high) - Rear Cross (low) - Jab (high)
- Jab (high) - Rear Cross (high) - Jab (high) - Rear Cross (high)
- Jab (high) - Jab (low) - Rear Cross (high)
- Jab (low) - Rear Cross (low) - Jab (low)
- Jab (high) - Rear Cross (high) - Lead Hook (high)
- Jab - (high) Rear Cross (high) - Lead Hook (low)
- Jab - Rear Cross - Lead Hook (high) - Rear Hook (high)
- Jab - Rear Cross - Lead Hook (low) - Rear Hook (low)
- Jab - Rear Cross - Lead Hook (high) - Rear Hook (low)
- Jab - Rear Cross - Lead Hook (low) - Rear Hook (high)
- Jab - Rear Hook (high)
- Jab - Rear Hook (low)

110

If you have a training partner, he can lend some assistance by holding the BOB while you strike it. This can be especially helpful because your partner can give you "real time" feedback while you are striking the bag.

- Jab - Lead Hook (high)

- Jab - Lead Hook (low)

- Jab - Lead Hook (high) - Rear hook (high)

- Jab - Lead Hook (low) - Rear hook (low)

- Jab - Lead Hook (high) - Rear hook (low)

- Jab - Lead Hook (low) - Rear hook (high)

- Jab - Jab - Rear Cross - Lead Hook (high)

- Jab - Jab - Rear Cross - Lead Hook (low)

- Jab - Rear Cross - Lead Hook (high) - Rear Uppercut

- Jab - Rear Cross - Lead Hook (high) - Rear Hook (low) - Lead Uppercut

- Rear Cross - Jab

- Rear Cross - Jab- Rear Cross

- Rear Cross - Jab- Rear Cross - Jab

- Rear Cross - Jab - Rear Hook (high)

- Rear Cross - Jab - Rear Hook (low)

- Rear Cross - Lead Hook (high)

- Rear Cross - Lead Hook (low)

- Rear Cross - Horizontal Elbow (front)

- Rear Cross - Horizontal Elbow (front) - Horizontal Elbow (rear)

- Rear Cross - Horizontal Elbow (front) - Horizontal Elbow (rear) - Diagonal Knee (front)

- Rear Cross - Lead Hook (high) - Rear Hook (high)

- Rear Cross - Lead Hook (low) - Rear Hook (low)

- Rear Cross - Lead Hook (high) - Rear Hook (low)

- Rear Cross - Lead Hook (low) - Rear Hook (high)

- Rear Cross - Lead Hook (high) - Rear Uppercut

- Rear Cross - Lead Hook (low) - Rear Uppercut

- Rear Cross - Lead Hook (high) - Rear Cross

- Rear Cross - Lead Hook (low) - Rear Cross

- Rear Uppercut - Lead Uppercut

- Rear Uppercut - Lead Uppercut - Rear Uppercut

- Rear Uppercut - Lead Uppercut -Rear Uppercut - Lead Uppercut

112

- Rear Uppercut - Lead Uppercut - Rear Hook - Lead Hook

- Rear Uppercut - Lead Hook (high)

- Rear Uppercut - Lead Hook (low)

- Rear Uppercut - Lead Hook (high) - Rear Hook (high)

- Rear Uppercut - Lead Hook (low) - Rear Hook (low)

- Rear Uppercut - Lead Hook (high) - Rear Hook (low)

- Rear Uppercut - Lead Hook (low) - Rear Hook (high)

Punching and Kicking Combinations

What follows are just a few punching and kicking combinations you can employ in your workouts:

- Jab - Hook Kick (rear leg)

- Jab - Jab - Hook Kick (rear leg)

- Jab - Rear Cross - Hook Kick (front leg)

- Jab - Rear Cross - Hook Kick (front leg) - Hook Kick (rear leg)

- Jab - Diagonal Knee (rear)

- Jab - Diagonal Knee (rear) - Diagonal Knee (front)

- Jab - Diagonal Knee (rear) - Horizontal elbow (front)

- Jab - Rear Cross - Diagonal Knee (front)

- Jab - Rear Cross - Push Kick (rear)

- Jab - Rear Cross - Jab - Rear Cross - Hook Kick (rear)

- Jab - Rear Cross - Jab - Rear Cross - Push Kick (rear)

- Jab - Rear Cross - Push Kick (rear) - Diagonal Knee (front)

- Jab - Rear Cross - Push Kick (rear) - Hook Kick (front)

- Jab - Rear Cross - Diagonal Knee (front) - Horizontal Elbow (rear)

113

- Push Kick (front leg) - Rear Cross (high)

- Push Kick (front leg) - Rear Cross (low)

- Push Kick (front leg) - Rear Cross (high) - Lead Hook (high)

- Push Kick (front leg) - Rear Cross (low) - Lead Hook (low)

- Push Kick (front leg) - Rear Cross (low) - Lead Hook (high)

- Push Kick (front leg) - Rear Cross (high) - Lead Hook (low)

- Push Kick (front leg) - Rear Cross (high) - Lead Hook (high) - Rear Hook (high)

- Push Kick (front leg) - Rear Cross (high) - Lead Hook (low) - Rear Hook (low)

- Push Kick (front leg) - Rear Uppercut

- Push Kick (front leg) - Rear Uppercut - Lead Uppercut

- Push Kick (front leg) - Rear Uppercut - Lead Uppercut - Diagonal Knee (rear)

- Hook Kick (front) - Rear Cross (high)

- Hook Kick (front) - Rear Cross (low)

- Hook Kick (front) - Rear Cross (high) - Lead Hook (high)

- Hook Kick (front) - Rear Cross (high) - Lead Hook (low)

- Hook Kick (front) - Rear Hook (high) - Rear Hook (high)

- Hook Kick (front) - Rear Hook (low) - Rear Hook (low)

- Hook Kick (front) - Rear Hook (high) - Rear Hook (low)

- Hook Kick (front) - Rear Hook (low) - Rear Hook (high)

- Side Kick (front) - Jab - Rear Cross

- Side Kick (front) - Jab - Rear Cross - Lead Hook

- Side Kick (front) - Rear Cross

- Side Kick (front) - Rear Cross - Lead Straight

- Side Kick (front) - Rear Cross - Horizontal Elbow (front)

- Side Kick (front) - Rear Cross - Horizontal Elbow (front) - Horizontal Elbow (rear)

- Side Kick (front) - Rear Cross - Hook Kick (front)

- Side Kick (front) - Diagonal Knee (rear)

- Side Kick (front) - Diagonal Knee (rear) - Horizontal Elbow (front)

Create Your Own Combinations

Use this section to write down your own body opponent bag combinations.

1.

2.

3.

4.

5.

6.

7.

8.

9.

10.

11.

12.

13.

14.

15.

16.

17.

18.

19.

29.

21.

22.

23.

24.

25.

26.

27.

28.

29.

30.

31.

32.

33.

34.

35.

36.

37.

38.

39.

40.

CHAPTER SEVEN
Advanced Workouts

Besides time-based workouts, there are a wide variety of advanced workouts and drills that can be performed on the body opponent bag. Some include:

- First strike training
- Punching proficiency training
- Compound attack training
- Multiple attacker drill
- Claustrophobic effect drill
- Swimming drill
- Isometric choke drill
- Pummeling drill
- Spooning drill
- Stick fighting training
- Stick strangles
- Knife fighting training
- Kubotan (mini stick) training
- BOB in the Middle drill
- Widowmaker "razing" skills

Let's take a look at just a few that you can add to your training.

First Strike Training

Because of it's realistic or lifelike facial features, the body opponent bag is ideal for developing your first strike skills. Essentially, a first strike is defined as the strategic application of proactive force designed to interrupt the initial stages of an assault before it becomes a self-defense situation.

This unique offensive strategy is crucial for self-defense because it allows you to incapacitate the opponent swiftly while at the same time precluding his capability to retaliate. No time is wasted, and no unnecessary risks are taken.

One inescapable fact about street combat is the longer the fight lasts, the greater your chances of serious injury or even death. Common sense suggests that you must end the street fight as quickly as possible.

The element of surprise is invaluable. Launching the first strike gives you the upper hand because it allows you to attack the adversary suddenly and unexpectedly. As a result, you demolish his defenses and ultimately take him out of the fight.

First Strike Techniques

First strike techniques are specific strikes designed to initiate a preemptive strike against your adversary. These techniques differ greatly from the punches and strikes discussed in the previous chapter. The following preemptive strikes are used for street self-defense applications because they are quick, destructive, and virtually non-telegraphic. Some include:

- Vertical Kick

- Push Kick

- Finger Jab

- Palm Heel Strike

- Short Arc Hammer Fist

- Knife Hand Strike

"When danger is imminent, strike first, strike fast, strike with authority and keep the pressure on."

First Strike Example #1

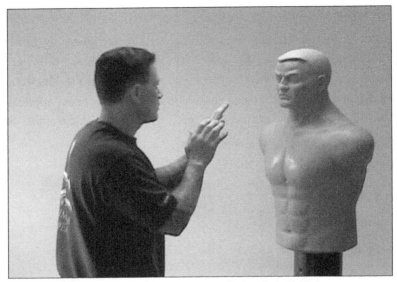

Here, the author assumes a first strike stance.

He delivers a rear palm heel to BOB's chin.

First Strike Example #2

The author assumes a first strike stance.

Without telegraphing his intentions, he delivers a quick finger jab strike to BOB's eyes.

First Strike Example #3

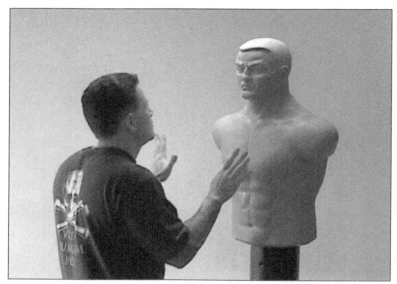

Mr. Franco squares off with the body opponent bag.

He launches a rear elbow strike to BOB's solar plexus.

124

The First Strike Workout Program

First Strike Techniques	Beginner	Intermediate	Advanced
Palm Heel to nose	25-50 reps	75-100 reps	200-500 reps
Palm Heel to chin	25-50 reps	75-100 reps	200-500 reps
Finger Jab to eyes	25-50 reps	75-100 reps	200-500 reps
Rear Elbow to sternum	25-50 reps	75-100 reps	200-500 reps
Rear Elbow to temple	25-50 reps	75-100 reps	200-500 reps

This program is designed to sharpen individual first strike techniques one at a time by executing it over and over for a prescribed number of repetitions.

Begin by performing the rep range associated with your skill level (i.e., beginner, intermediate and advanced). For example, a beginner level practitioner would perform between 25-50 repetitions for each first strike technique (twenty-five being the minimum amount of repetitions and fifty being the maximum).

Everyone should start at the beginner level and work from there. Warning! Regardless of your conditioning level or experience, never start at the Intermediate or Advanced levels.

First Month Routine:

For the entire first month, perform each of the first strike techniques from a right first strike stance only.

Second Month Routine:

For the entire second month, perform each of the first strike techniques from a left first strike stance only.

Third Month Routine:

For the entire third month execute half of your repetitions from your right stance and the remaining half from your left stance.

Fourth Month Routine:

For the entire fourth month, perform the maximum rep range for each technique and from each stance. For example, if you are training at the intermediate level you would be performing 100 reps for both the right and left stances, totaling 200 repetitions for each first strike technique. So your total repetition count for all six techniques would be 1,200 for a complete workout.

Fifth Month Routine:

Depending on your level of conditioning and mastery of the techniques, beginners may continue to the intermediate level workout and follow it for the next four months. Intermediate practitioners can move up to the advanced level program and follow it for the next four months. However, if you think you're not ready to move up to the next level or just don't feel that you're "fluid" with the body mechanics, you can remain at your current training level indefinitely. Use your best judgment and take your time. Remember, it's not a race!

A Word About Advanced Level Training:

The advanced level should only be performed after you have been training regularly for one full year. Take my word; it's a brutal level of training reserved for the most diehard practitioner!

More tips: To avoid injury and burnout, do not workout more than two times per week. Be patient and allow your body to adapt to the stress and demands of the training. Proficiency training should never be a "cardio" or time based workout. If you are out of breath during the exercise, then you are performing the repetitions too fast. Remember to take your time between each repetition!

Also remember to perform all first strike techniques from a solid first strike stance. If you need more information about the first strike methodology, you might want to read First Strike: Mastering the Preemptive Strike for Street Combat, available on Amazon.com

126

Punching Proficiency Training

Techniques	Beginner	Intermediate	Advanced
Jab	25-50 reps	75-100 reps	200-500 reps
Rear Cross Punch	25-50 reps	75-100 reps	200-500 reps
Lead Hook Punch	25-50 reps	75-100 reps	200-500 reps
Rear Hook Punch	25-50 reps	75-100 reps	200-500 reps
Lead Uppercut	25-50 reps	75-100 reps	200-500 reps
Rear Uppercut	25-50 reps	75-100 reps	200-500 reps
Lead Elbow Strike	25-50 reps	75-100 reps	200-500 reps
Rear Elbow Strike	25-50 reps	75-100 reps	200-500 reps

Punching proficiency training will sharpen individual punches one at a time by executing it over and over for a prescribed number of repetitions.

Begin the program by performing the rep range associated with your skill level (i.e., beginner, intermediate and advanced). For example, a beginner level practitioner would perform between 25-50 repetitions for each conventional punch (twenty-five being the minimum amount of repetitions and fifty being the maximum).

Everyone should start at the beginner level and work from there. Warning! Regardless of your conditioning level or experience, never start at the Intermediate or Advanced levels.

First Month Routine:

For the entire first month, perform each conventional punch from a right fighting stance only.

Second Month Routine:

For the entire second month, perform each conventional punch from a left fighting stance only.

Third Month Routine:

For the entire third month execute half of your repetitions from your right stance and the remaining half from your left stance.

Fourth Month Routine:

For the entire fourth month, perform the maximum rep range for each technique and from each stance. For example, if you are training at the intermediate level you would be performing 100 reps for both the right and left stances, totaling 200 repetitions for each technique. So your total repetition count for all six techniques would be 1,600 for a complete workout.

Fifth Month Workout Routine:

Depending on your level of conditioning and mastery of the techniques, beginners may continue to the intermediate level workout and follow it for the next four months. Intermediate practitioners can move up to the advanced level program and follow it for the next four months. However, if you think you're not ready to move up to the next level or just don't feel that you're "fluid" with the body mechanics, you can remain at your current training level indefinitely.

Advanced Level Training:

The advanced level should only be performed after you have been training regularly for one full year.

Punching proficiency training means performing one technique at a time for a set number or repetitions. Here, the author performs a rear hook punch to BOB's head.

Compound Attack Training

Combination Sequence	Beginner	Intermediate	Advanced
JB - RC	25-50 reps	75-100 reps	150-250 reps
JB – RC – JB - RC	25-50 reps	75-100 reps	150-250 reps
JB – RC – LH - RH	25-50 reps	75-100 reps	150-250 reps
JB – RH – LH - RH	25-50 reps	75-100 reps	150-250 reps
LH – RH – LH - RH	25-50 reps	75-100 reps	150-250 reps
JB – RC – LUC	25-50 reps	75-100 reps	150-250 reps
RC – LH – RUC	25-50 reps	75-100 reps	150-250 reps
LE - RE	25-50 reps	75-100 reps	150-250 reps
RE - LE - RE - LE	25-50 reps	75-100 reps	150-250 reps

Technique Legend:
JB = Jab
RC = Rear Cross Punch
LH = Lead Hook Punch
RH = Rear Hook Punch
LUC = Lead Uppercut
RUC = Rear Uppercut
LE = Lead Elbow
RE = Rear Elbow

I mentioned earlier that a "compound attack" is the logical sequence of two or more techniques thrown in strategic succession. In this workout program, you perform a specific combination for a prescribed number of repetitions.

To start, perform the rep range associated with your skill level (i.e., beginner, intermediate and advanced). For example, a beginner level practitioner would perform between 25-50 repetitions for each combination (twenty-five being the minimum amount of repetitions and fifty being the maximum). Remember, each combination sequence counts as one repetition.

Everyone should start at the beginner level and work from there. Warning! Regardless of your conditioning level or experience, never start at the Intermediate or Advanced levels.

First Month Routine:

For the entire first month, perform each combination sequence from a right stance only.

Second Month Routine:

For the entire second month, perform each combination sequence from a left stance only.

Third Month Routine:

For the entire third month execute half of your repetitions from your right stance and the remaining half from your left stance.

Fourth Month Routine:

For the entire fourth month, perform the maximum rep range for each combination sequence and from each stance. For example, if you are training at the intermediate level you would be performing 100 combination sequences for both the right and left stances, totaling 200 repetitions for each combination sequence. So your total repetition count for all nine combination sequences would be 1,800 for a complete workout.

Fifth Month Routine:

Depending on your level of conditioning and mastery of the techniques, beginners may continue to the intermediate level workout and follow it for the next four months. Intermediate practitioners can move up to the advanced level program and follow it for the next four months. However, if you think you're not ready to move up to the next level or just don't feel that you're "fluid" with the body mechanics, you can remain at your current training level indefinitely. Use your best judgment and take your time. Remember, it's not a race!

Advanced Level Training:

The advanced level should only be performed after you have been training regularly for one full year.

Pummeling Drill

Technique	Beginner	Intermediate	Advanced
Linear Blast	4 sets 30-45 seconds	6 sets 60-90 seconds	8 sets 120-180 seconds
Short Arc Hammer Fist	4 sets 30-45 seconds	6 sets 60-90 seconds	8 sets 120-180 seconds

The body opponent bag can also be used for improving your ground fighting skills, including pummeling. Essentially, pummeling is strategically punching the adversary from the top mounted position. There are two punches that can be delivered effectively from this position. They are:

- Linear blast

- Short Arc Hammer Fist

When performing both punches, remember to keep everything tight and aim for BOBs face, specifically his nose or chin. You objective is to punch through your target while avoiding type of jabbing motion. When pummeling the body opponent bag you can vary the cadence to the punches from moderate to full speed.

Pummeling is a devastating self-defense technique that can severely injure your adversary and should only be used in life and death situations. Remember to always be certain that your actions are legally and morally justified in the eyes of the law.

The Pummeling Program

Perform the techniques for the time range associated with your skill level (i.e., beginner, intermediate and advanced). For example, a beginner level practitioner would perform each pummeling technique for 30 to 45 seconds. He would rest for a brief amount of time and then perform the same technique again for a total of four times or four sets.

Important: You'll notice the pummeling drill is conducted for a prolonged or exaggerated amount of time. This is done strictly for body mechanic mastery as well as muscular endurance. Never, ever apply pummeling technique for a prolonged amount of time against a human being. Doing so can cause brain damage or death for your adversary.

First Month Routine:

For the entire first month, perform each pummeling technique as a single blow with the right hand only.

Second Month Routine:

For the entire second month, perform each pummeling technique as a single blow with the left hand only.

Third Month Routine:

For the entire third month execute half of your sets from your right hand and the remaining half from your left hand.

Fourth Month Routine:

For the entire fourth month, perform each pummeling technique back and forth with both your right and left hands for the maximum time range. For example, if you are training at the intermediate level you would be performing six sets for both the right and left hands.

Fifth Month Routine:

Depending on your level of conditioning and mastery of the technique, beginners may continue to the intermediate level workout and follow it for the next four months. Intermediate practitioners can move up to the advanced level program and follow it for the next four months.

"The pummeling drill is conducted for a prolonged amount of time. This is done strictly for body mechanic mastery and muscular endurance. Never, ever apply pummeling technique for a prolonged amount of time against a human being. Doing so can cause brain damage or death."

Pictured here, the author demonstrates a linear blast to the body opponent bag. Notice how is other hand is loaded and ready to deliver the next shot.

Pummeling Example

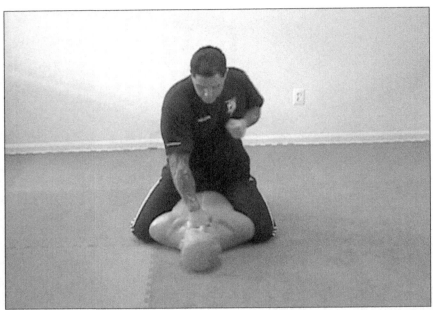

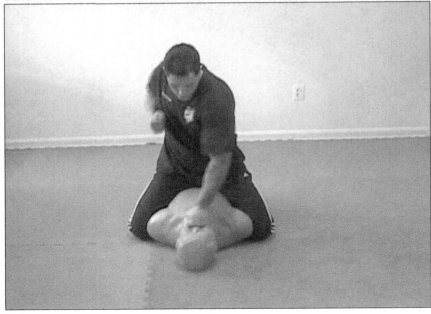

You can also add elbow strikes to the pummeling drill. In this photo, the practitioner performs a descending elbow strike to the body opponent bag.

Spooning Drill

The spooning drill is an advanced isometric exercise that develops the rear naked choke, the leg scissors hold as well as overall combat endurance.

To successfully perform this exercise you will first need to remove the torso of the BOB from the stem. You will also need a minimum of two people. One man to spoon the body opponent bag, and the other to twist, turn and roll the torso in different directions.

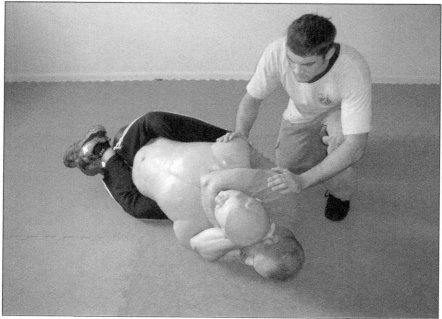

The spooning drill can be very taxing on the practitioner and should only be performed by intermediate grapplers who have a strong foundation in ground fighting.

The Spooning Program

Technique	Beginner	Intermediate	Advanced
Right Rear Naked Choke	4 sets 15-30 seconds	6 sets 45-60 seconds	8 sets 90-120 seconds
Left Rear Naked Choke	4 sets 15-30 seconds	6 sets 45-60 seconds	8 sets 90-120 seconds

Perform the choke for the time range associated with your skill level (i.e., beginner, intermediate and advanced). For example, a beginner level practitioner would choke the Body Opponent Bag between 15 to 30 seconds. He would rest for a brief period of time and then perform the choke again for the required amount of time. He would do this for a total of four times or four sets.

Warning! Never perform the spooning drill on a live person, death or serious bodily harm may occur. This exercise routine is exclusively for the body opponent bag.

Important: The spooning drill requires you to apply and maintain the rear naked choke technique for a prolonged amount of time. This is done strictly for body mechanic mastery and muscular endurance. Never, ever apply choking techniques for a prolonged amount of time against a human being. Doing so can cause brain damage or death for your adversary.

First Month Routine:

For the entire first month, perform the right arm naked choke only.

Second Month Routine:

For the entire second month, perform the left arm naked choke only.

Third Month Routine:

For the entire third month execute half of your sets with a right arm rear naked choke and the remaining half with a left arm rear naked choke.

Fourth Month Routine:

For the entire fourth month, perform the maximum time range for both the right and left rear named choke. For example, if you are training at the intermediate level you would be performing six sets for both the right and left choke, with 60 seconds hold per set.

Fifth Month Routine:

Depending on your level of conditioning and mastery of the choke, beginners may continue to the intermediate level workout and follow it for the next four months. Intermediate practitioners can move up to the advanced level program and follow it for the next four months.

However, if you think you're not ready to move up to the next level or just don't feel that you're "fluid" with the body mechanics, you can remain at your current training level indefinitely.

"The spooning drill is an advanced isometric exercise that develops the rear naked choke, the leg scissors hold as well as overall combat endurance."

Stick & Knife Training

Again, because the body opponent bag has lifelike anatomical features, it's the ideal training tool for hand-held weapons training such as knife and stick fighting. This is especially helpful for people who study Filipino martial arts (FMA) like Kali, Arnis or Escrima.

Combination Sequence	Beginner	Intermediate	Advanced
A1 – A2	25-50 reps	75-100 reps	200-500 reps
A3 – A4	25-50 reps	75-100 reps	200-500 reps
A5 - A6	25-50 reps	75-100 reps	200-500 reps
A7 High - A7 Low	25-50 reps	75-100 reps	200-500 reps
A1 - A2 - A3 - A4	25-50 reps	75-100 reps	200-500 reps
A8 – A9	25-50 reps	75-100 reps	200-500 reps
A1 – A2 – A3 – A4 – A5 – A6 – A7 – A8 – A9	25-50 reps	75-100 reps	200-500 reps

Technique Legend

Note: The following angles of attack can apply to both the knife or stick.

A1 = Angle 1 is a diagonal forehand strike traveling right to left.

A2 = Angle 2 is a diagonal backhand strike traveling left to right.

A3 = Angle 3 is a horizontal forehand strike traveling right to left.

A4 = Angle 4 is a horizontal backhand strike traveling left to right.

A5 = Angle 5 is an upward diagonal forehand strike moving right to left.

A6 = Angle 6 is an upward diagonal backhand strike moving left to right.

A7 = Angle 7 is a linear thrust

A8 = Angle 8 is a downward vertical strike

A9 = Angle 9 is an upwards vertical strike.

Perform the rep range associated with your skill level (i.e., beginner, intermediate and advanced). For example, a beginner level practitioner would perform between 25-50 repetitions for each combination (twenty-five being the minimum amount of repetitions and fifty being the maximum). Remember, each combination sequence counts as one repetition.

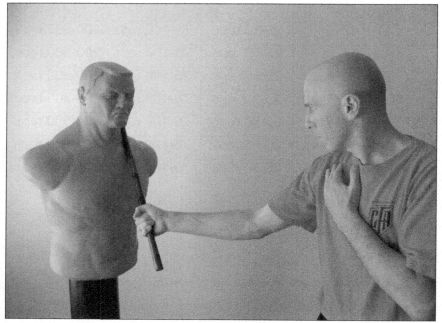

Pictured here, the practitioner hits the body opponent bag with an angle one strike to the collar bone.

First Month Routine:

For the entire first month, perform each combination sequence with your right hand only.

142

Second Month Routine:

For the entire second month, perform each combination sequence with your left hand only.

Third Month Routine:

For the entire third month execute half of your repetitions with your right hand and the remaining half from your left hand.

Fourth Month Routine:

For the entire fourth month, perform the maximum rep range for each combination sequence and from each hand. For example, if you are training at the intermediate level you would be performing 100 combination sequences for both the right and left hands, totaling 200 repetitions for each combination sequence. So your total repetition count for all seven combination sequences would be 1,400 for a complete workout.

Fifth Month Routine:

Depending on your level of conditioning and mastery of the techniques, beginners may continue to the intermediate level workout and follow it for the next four months. Intermediate practitioners can move up to the advanced level program and follow it for the next four months. However, if you think you're not ready to move up to the next level or just don't feel that you're "fluid" with the body mechanics, you can remain at your current training level indefinitely.

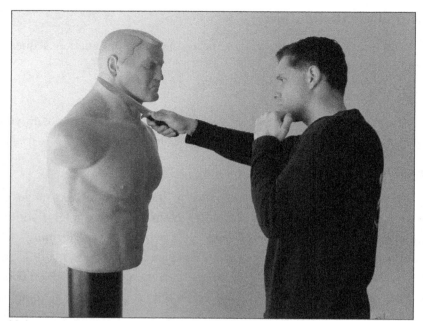

Make certain to only use training knives when working out on the body opponent bag. In this photo, the author perform an angle two cut on the body opponent bag.

Only use rattan training stick when working out on the body opponent bag.

144

The Widow Maker Program

I early 2003, I created a very unique method of close-quarter fighting called the Widow Maker program. This uncommon fighting style was specifically designed to provide law-abiding citizens with lethal force techniques when faced with immediate threat of an unlawful deadly criminal attack. The Widow Maker program is divided into two phases: Webbing and Razing

Webbing

At first glance, the webbing technique looks like a reinforced palm heel strike delivered to the assailant's chin. It is termed Webbing because your hands resemble a large web that wraps around the enemy's face.

The Webbing strike, however, is not just a matter of simply launching a double palm heel strike at the opponent. There is much more to it than that. Webbing requires specific hand and arm articulation, proper body mechanics and correct timing.

However, once mastered, Webbing will feel natural and will become an instinctual body weapon that can be deployed under the stress of a deadly criminal attack.

Razing

Razing, on the other hand, is the second phase of the program and it involves a series of vicious close-quarter techniques designed to physically and psychologically incapacitate a criminal attacker.

These close-quarter techniques are executed at various beats (half beat, quarter beat and zero beat) and they include: eye raking, gouging, tearing, crushing, biting, hair pulling, elbow strikes, head butts, bicep pops, neck cranks, shaving forearms, and finishing chokes.

Unfortunately, it would take an entire book to adequately teach you the Widow Maker methodology, but the point I want to make is the body opponent bag is the only training tool available for developing both Webbing and Razing skills.

Razing on the Body Opponent Bag

For those of you who are familiar with the Widow Maker program, here are some important tips when training on the body opponent bag:

1. When working on the body opponent bag, don't "force the raze." Let your series of techniques flow naturally and easily. If you are having trouble, consider applying petroleum jelly to face of the body opponent bag. This will help facilitate speed with your quarter beat techniques.

2. Switch right and left anchors frequently when Razing the BOB.

3. Don't forget to add biting tactics in the course of your compound attack. Just be careful not to puncture the BOB.

4. Always remain relaxed when razing the bag. Tightening your muscles will only slow you down and break your offensive flow.

5. Get into the habit of executing "zero beat" techniques at the end of your sequence of hits.

6. Practice your razing skills on the body opponent bag at least three times per week (30 minutes per workout) for six consecutive months.

7. Keep your Razing movement "clean" and "tight", avoid sloppy telegraphic movements.

8. While the Body Opponent Bag is a good training tool, understand and recognize its inherent limitations. Remember, razing

146

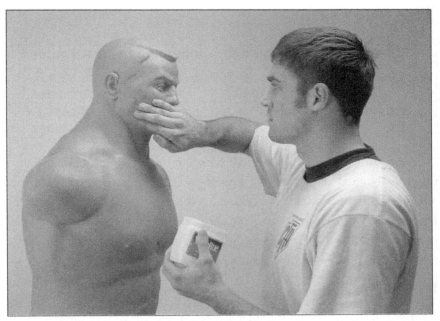

If you want to improve the speed and overall flow of your razing techniques, you can apply petroleum jelly to BOB's face.

a stationary mannequin bag is nothing like Razing an adrenaline induced human being.

9.   Remember to breath when attacking the bag. Breathing is one of the most important and often neglected aspects of razing. Proper breathing promotes muscular relaxation and increases the speed and efficiency of your compound attack. The rate at which you breath will also determine how quickly your cardiorespiratory system can recover from the fight.

10. Never stand squarely in front of the body opponent bag when razing. Use your footwork and move around as you attack.

The Program

Technique	Beginner	Intermediate	Advanced
Right Hand Razing	4 sets 15-30 seconds	6 sets 60-90 seconds	8 sets 2-4 minutes
Left Hand Razing	4 sets 15-30 seconds	6 sets 60-90 seconds	8 sets 2-4 minutes

Perform the razing methodology on the body opponent for the time range associated with your skill level (i.e., beginner, intermediate and advanced). For example, a beginner level practitioner would raze the Body Opponent Bag between 15 to 30 seconds. He would rest for a brief period of time and then raze again for the required amount of time. He would do this for a total of four times or four sets.

First Month Routine:

For the entire first month, raze the BOB with your right hand only.

Second Month Routine:

For the entire second month, raze the BOB with your left hand only.

Third Month Routine:

For the entire third month execute half of your sets with the right hand and the remaining half with the left hand.

Fourth Month Routine

For the entire fourth month, perform the maximum time range for both the right and left hands. For example, if you are training at the intermediate level you would be performing six sets for both the right and left hands, for a duration on 90 seconds.

Fifth Month Routine

Depending on your level of conditioning and mastery of the choke, beginners may proceed to the intermediate level workout and follow it for the next four months. Intermediate practitioners can move up to the advanced level program and follow it for the next four months. However, if you think you're not ready to move up to the next level or just don't feel that you're "fluid" with the body mechanics, you can remain at your current training level indefinitely.

Warning! Never practice the razing technique on a live person, serious bodily harm may occur. This exercise routine is exclusively for the body opponent bag.

Webbing Demonstration

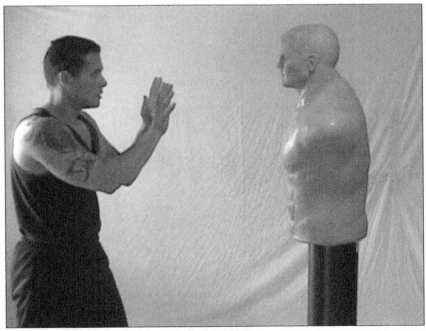

In this photo, the author prepares to launch a webbing strike to the body opponent bag.

Pictured here, Mr. Franco closes the distance gap with a webbing strike to BOB's chin.

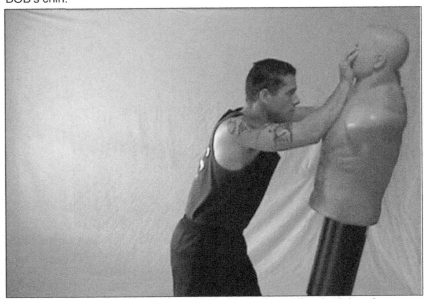

Once the two hands make solid contact with the bag, allow both hands to split apart. Your left hand grasps the nape of BOB's neck (this is called anchoring) while the right hand begins to raze his face.

150

Razing Demonstration

Once you have landed the webbing strike and have successfully anchored the body opponent bag, you must immediately flow into the razing method of attack. Again, it's critical that you don't permit your offensive flow to break for even a second.

The key objective is to harmoniously amalgamate webbing and razing into one relentless and strategically calculated assault. In turn, this will "freeze out" the enemy's cognitive brain function. Essentially, he's screwed!

Of all methods of unarmed combat, razing is without question the most vicious. Its feral and brutal characteristics are both psychologically and physically traumatic for the adversary. The overwhelming nature of razing invokes instantaneous terror by delivering a destructiveness exceeding that of a deadly and evil criminal aggressor.

Unfortunately, still photographs don't do justice to the razing method of fighting. However, here are just a few razing techniques that can be applied to the body opponent bag.

Eye Rakes

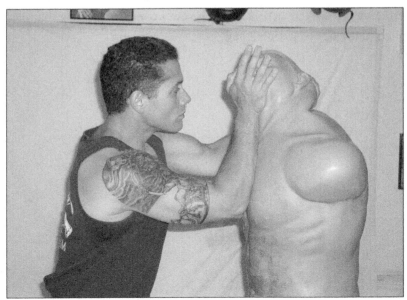

Neck Cranks

Shaving Forearms

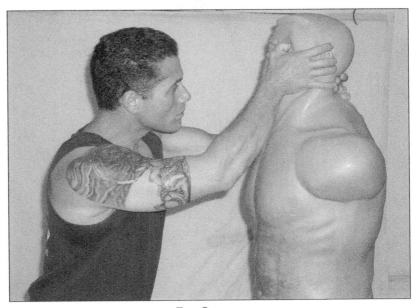

Eye Gouges

153

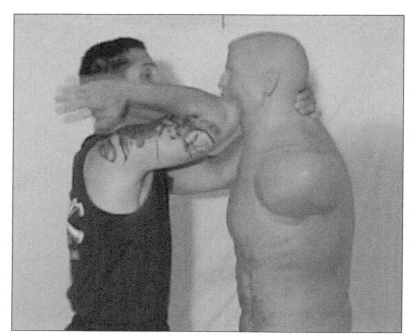

Vertical Elbows

Biting

154

"Of all methods of unarmed fighting, razing is without question the most vicious. Its feral and brutal characteristics are both psychologically and physically traumatic for the adversary. The overwhelming nature of razing invokes instantaneous terror by delivering a destructiveness exceeding that of a criminal aggressor."

More Drills

There are countless other drills that can be performed on the body opponent bag. Frankly, you are only limited by your own imagination.. Here, are a few more.

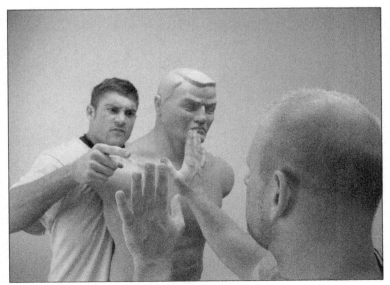

BOB in the Middle Drill

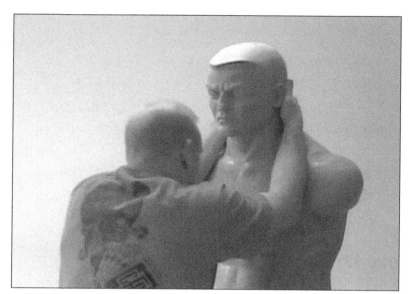

The Clinch Drill

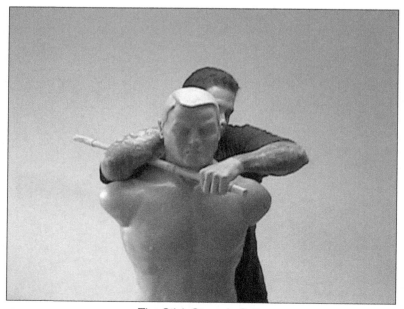

The Stick Strangle Drill

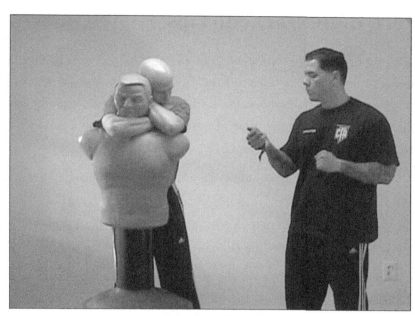

Isometric Choke Drill

Multiple Attackers Drills

157

More BOB Workout Tips

- Before you begin your workout program, make certain that you have been cleared by your doctor. Since there is always some risk involved in training and because each person is unique, it is important that before beginning any type of training program, you should have a complete physical examination by your physician.

- Before hitting the bag, always warm up with some light stretching and calisthenics.

- Always start your first round on the bag with light punches and kicks. Never go all out in the beginning of your workout session.

- When hitting the bag, never sacrifice proper technique for power or speed.

- Always throw your punching or kicking techniques from a good fighting stance.

- Don't chew gum when working out on the bag.

- Avoid wearing watches and jewelry when training.

- Consider shadow boxing with light dumbbells to strengthen your arm and shoulders for bag work.

- Never hold your breath. Remember to exhale with the delivery of every technique.

- Before you invest your time and money in a body opponent bag program, it's important to first define your goals. What do you hope to accomplish by training on the bag? For example, do you want to get in better shape? Build up your confidence? Handle a vicious street thug? Enter a mixed martial arts competition?

- Be cognizant of your distance from the bag always. Stand too close when punching the bag will result in a "pushing effect" while standing too far will just cause the punch to simply glance the target.

- When working out alone, avoid the urge to stop the bag from moving. Let it swing!

- Avoid the habit of tapping your gloves together before delivering a punch on the bag.

- If you don't know the proper way to throw a punch or kick, get instruction from a qualified coach or instructor.

- Avoid locking out your elbows when punching the bag.

- Be mobile when working out on the bag, avoid the tendency to just stand and punch.

- Avoid premature exhaustion by pacing yourself during your bag workouts.

- The BOB doesn't hit back, so be aware of your own target openings and vulnerabilities when hitting the bag.

- Never let children play or swing from the bag.

- Remember to maintain your balance always when punching the bag - never sacrifice your balance for power.

- The BOB can be unforgiving on your body and will certainly test the structural integrity of you punches and blows. Please remember to keep your wrists straight when your fists hit the bag. Learn to gradually build up the force of your blows - a beginner's wrists are generally too weak to accommodate full force strikes on the punching bag.

- When using the body opponent bag, learn to relax and avoid unnecessarily tensing your arm and shoulder muscles. Muscular tension will throw off the timing of your punches, retard the speed of your blows, kicks and strikes and most certainly wear you out during your workout.

• Punching bags often cause fighters to "lose their form" when delivering their blows. Try to be constantly aware of your form when hitting the bag or better yet have a training partner, teacher or coach observe you when working out on the bag. Another suggestion is to video tape yourself using the punching bag. This will give you a good idea of what you are doing in your workouts.

• Remember to maintain your balance at all times when punching the bag - never sacrifice your balance for power.

• Avoid bag training two days in a row. Give your body a few days to recover from your last workout.

• To avoid injury or burn out, don't engage in BOB training more than three times per week.

• Get into the habit of regularly inspecting your bag for tears and other signs of wear.

• Avoid the latest gimmicks - Every so often, some cleaver marketing company will come up with a trendy gimmick that can be added to your workouts. Keep your punching bag workouts plain and simple. Beginners should avoid adding hand weights, weighted bag gloves, resistance bands and elevations masks to their workouts.

• While many people use the body opponent bag for boxing, kick boxing and mixed martial arts training, don't forget the BOB is a fantastic tool for developing effective self-defense techniques.

• Remember that BOB training for combat sports is much different from heavy bag training for real world self-defense scenarios.

• Unless you are highly skilled martial artist, do not kick a body opponent bag while bare foot.

• Stay hydrated when working out on the bag. Dehydration can have a real negative effect on your workout, and it can also be dangerous. When working out, always drink plenty of water. Always hydrate before your workout by drinking at least one pint of water. During the summer months, drink more water than usual. Also get into the habit of taking a water bottle with you to your workouts.

• When buying gear, spare no expense. Body opponent bag training is a serious matter, and your training gear should reflect it. Good equipment will provide years of reliable use and enhance your fighting skills.

• Consider working out with music. Actually, your workouts can be dramatically enhanced by training to music. It's my experience that training to fast, rhythmic music works wonders for conditioning training, while hard-driving aggressive rock music works best for proficiency and street training methods.

BOB Maintenance

The body opponent bag is a low maintenance piece of equipment that will last for years if you take care of it. What follows are a few tips to help keep it in good working condition.

- Use soap and water to clean the torso, stem and base of the bag. Avoid using strong detergents and cleaners.

- If the skin of the mannequin develops a tear, try repairing it with vinyl adhesive that is available at most hardware stores.

- Avoid exposing the body opponent bag to extreme temperatures.

- Keep the torso away from direct sunlight for extended periods of time.

- If you must keep the bag outdoors, keep it away from the elements such as tree sap, or bird droppings.

- Always keep the base of the bag on a flat level surface .

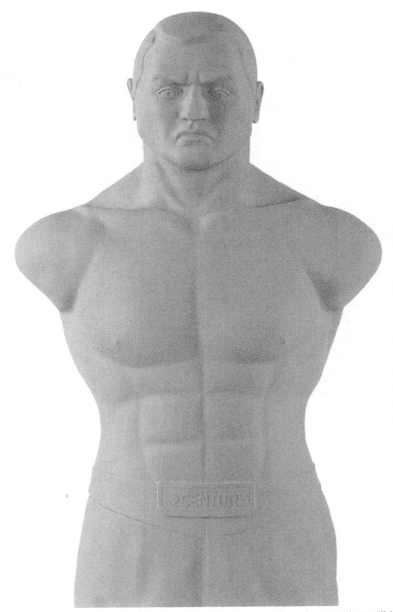

The body opponent bag is a low maintenance piece of equipment that will last for years if you take care of it.

168

Glossary

The following terms are defined in the context of Contemporary Fighting Arts and its related concepts. In many instances, the definitions bear little resemblance to those found in a standard dictionary.

A

Accuracy - The precise or exact projection of force. Accuracy is also defined as the ability to execute a combative movement with precision and exactness.

Adaptability - The ability to physically and psychologically adjust to new or different conditions or circumstances of combat.

Aerobic Exercise - "With air." Exercise that elevates the heart rate to a training level for a prolonged period of time, usually 30 minutes.

Agility - An attribute of combat. One's ability to move his or her body quickly and gracefully.

Ambidextrous - The ability to perform with equal facility on both the right and left sides of the body.

Attributes of Combat - The physical, mental, and spiritual qualities that enhance combat skills and tactics.

B

Balance - One's ability to maintain equilibrium while stationary or moving.

Blading the Body - Strategically positioning your body at a 45-degree angle.

BOB - (See body opponent bag.)

Body Mechanics - Technically precise body movement during the execution of a body weapon, defensive technique, or other fighting maneuver.

Body Opponent Bag - (also known as BOB). A self standing, body-shaped punching bag constructed of synthetic rubber material called plastisol. The body opponent bag is comprised of two separate parts: the torso and base.

Body Weapon - (also known as tool). One of the various body parts that can be used to strike or otherwise injure or kill a criminal assailant.

Burn Out – A negative emotional state acquired by physically over training. Some symptoms include: illness, boredom, anxiety, disinterest in training, and general sluggishness.

C

Cadence - Coordinating tempo and rhythm to establish a timing pattern of movement.

Cardiorespiratory Conditioning - The component of physical fitness that deals with the heart, lungs, and circulatory system.

Centerline - An imaginary vertical line that divides your body in half and which contains many of your vital anatomical targets.

Circular Movement - Movements that follow the direction of a curve.

Clinching - Strategically locking up with the adversary while you are standing.

Close Quarter Combat - One of the three ranges of knife and bludgeon combat. At this distance, you can strike, slash, or stab your assailant with a variety of close-quarter techniques.

Cognitive Development - One of the five elements of CFA's mental component. The process of developing and enhancing your fighting skills through specific mental exercises and techniques. (See analysis and integration, killer instinct, philosophy and strategic/tactical development.)

Combat Oriented Training – Training that is specifically related to the harsh realities of both armed and unarmed combat. (see ritual oriented training and sport oriented training.)

Combative Arts - The various arts of war. (See martial arts.)

Combative Attributes - (See attributes of combat.)

Combative Fitness - A state characterized by cardiorespiratory and muscular/skeletal conditioning, as well as proper body composition.

Combat Ranges - The various ranges of unarmed combat.

Combative Utility - The quality of condition of being combatively useful.

Combination(s) - (See compound attack.)

Compound Attack - One of the five conventional methods of attack. Two or more body weapons launched in strategic succession whereby the fighter overwhelms his assailant with a flurry of full speed, full force blows.

Conditioning Training - A CFA training methodology requiring the practitioner to deliver a variety of offensive and defensive combinations for a four minute period (See proficiency training and street training.)

Contemporary Fighting Arts® (CFA) - A modern martial art and self-defense system made up of three parts: physical, mental, and spiritual.

Coordination - A physical attribute characterized by the ability to perform a technique or movement with efficiency, balance, and accuracy.

Counterattack - Offensive action made to counter an assailant's initial attack.

Cross Stepping - The process of crossing one foot in front or behind the other when moving.

D

Defense - The ability to strategically thwart an assailant's attack (armed or unarmed).

Diet - A life-style of healthy eating.

Distancing - The ability to quickly understand spatial relationships and how they relate to combat.

Double-End Bag – A small leather ball suspended in the air by bungee cord which develops striking accuracy, speed, timing, eye-hand coordination, footwork and overall defensive skills.

E

Effectiveness - One of the three criteria for a CFA body weapon, technique, tactic or maneuver. It means the ability to produce a desired effect (See efficiency and safety.)

Efficiency - One of the three criteria for a CFA body weapon, technique, tactic or maneuver. It means the ability to reach an objective quickly and economically (see effectiveness and safety.)

Evasion - A defensive maneuver that allows you to strategically maneuver your body away from the assailant's strike.

Evasive Sidestepping - Evasive footwork where the practitioner moves to either the right or left side.

Evasiveness - A combative attribute. The ability of avoid threat or danger.

Excessive Force - An amount of force that exceeds the need for a particular event and is unjustified in the eyes of the law.

Experimentation - The painstaking process of testing a combative hypothesis or theory.

Explosiveness - A combative attribute that is characterized by a sudden outburst of violent energy.

F

Fighting Stance - One of the different types of stances used in CFA's system. A strategic posture you can assume when face-to-face with an unarmed assailant (s). The fighting stance is generally used after you have launched your first strike tool.

Finesse - A combative attribute. The ability to skillfully execute a movement or a series of movements with grace and refinement.

Fisted blows – Hand blows delivered with a clenched fist.

Flexibility - The muscles' ability to move through maximum natural ranges (See muscular/skeletal conditioning.)

Focus Mitts – Durable leather hands mitts used to develop and sharpen offensive and defensive skills.

Footwork - Quick, economical steps performed on the balls of the feet while you are relaxed, alert, and balanced. Footwork is structured around four general movements: forward, backward, right, and left.

G

Grappling Range - One of the three ranges of unarmed combat. Grappling range is the closest distance of unarmed combat from which you can employ a wide variety of close-quarter tools and techniques. The grappling range of unarmed combat is also divided into two different planes: vertical (standing) and horizontal (ground fighting). (See kicking range and punching range.)

Grappling Range Tools - The various body tools and techniques that are employed in the grappling range of unarmed combat, including head butts; biting, tearing, clawing, crushing, and gouging tactics; foot stomps, horizontal, vertical, and diagonal elbow strikes, vertical and diagonal knee strikes, chokes, strangles, joint locks, and holds. (See punching range tools and kicking range tools.)

H

Hand Positioning - (See guard.)

Hand Wraps – Long strips of cotton that are wrapped around the hands and wrists for greater protection.

Head-Hunter - A fighter who primarily attacks the head.

Heavy Bag - A large cylindrical shaped bag that is used to develop kicking, punching or striking power.

High-Line Kick - One of the two different classifications of a kick. A kick that is directed to targets above an assailant's waist level. (See low-line kick.)

Hook Kick - A circular kick that can be delivered in both kicking and punching ranges.

Hook Punch - A circular punch that can be delivered in both the punching and grappling ranges.

I

Impact Power - Destructive force generated by mass and velocity.

Incapacitate - To disable an assailant by rendering him unconscious or damaging his bones, joints or organs.

J

Jiu-jitsu – Translates to "soft/pliable". Jiu-jitsu is a martial art developed in feudal Japan that emphasizes throws, joint locks and weapons training.

Joint Lock - A grappling range technique that immobilizes the assailant's joint.

Judo - Translates to "gentle/soft way". Judo is an Olympic sport which originated in Japan.

K

Kick - A sudden, forceful strike with the foot.

Kicking Range - One of the three ranges of unarmed combat. Kicking range is the furthest distance of unarmed combat wherein you use your legs to strike an assailant. (See grappling range and punching range.)

Kicking Range Tools - The various body weapons employed in the kicking range of unarmed combat, including side kicks, push kicks, hook kicks, and vertical kicks.

L

Lead Side -The side of the body that faces an assailant.

Linear Movement - Movements that follow the path of a straight line.

Low Maintenance Tool - Offensive and defensive tools that require the least amount of training and practice to maintain proficiency. Low maintenance tools generally do not require preliminary stretching.

Low-Line Kick - One of the two different classifications of a kick. A kick that is directed to targets below the assailant's waist level. (See high-line kick.)

Lock - (See joint lock.)

M

Maneuver - To manipulate into a strategically desired position.

Martial arts - The "arts of war".

Mechanics - (See body mechanics.)

Mental Attributes - The various cognitive qualities that enhance your fighting skills.

Mental Component - One of the three vital components of the CFA system. The mental component includes the cerebral aspects of fighting including the Killer Instinct, Strategic & Tactical Development, Analysis & Integration, Philosophy and Cognitive Development (See physical component and spiritual component.)

Mixed Martial Arts - Also known as MMA, is a concept of fighting where the practitioner integrates a variety of fighting styles into a single method of fighting that can be tested in a regulated full-contact combat sport.

Mobility - A combative attribute. The ability to move your body quickly and freely while balanced. (See footwork.)

Modern Martial Art - A pragmatic combat art that has evolved to meet the demands and characteristics of the present time.

Muscular Endurance - The muscles' ability to perform the same motion or task repeatedly for a prolonged period of time.

Muscular Flexibility - The muscles' ability to move through maximum natural ranges.

Muscular Strength - The maximum force that can be exerted by a particular muscle or muscle group against resistance.

Muscular/Skeletal Conditioning - An element of physical fitness that entails muscular strength, endurance, and flexibility.

N

Neutral Zone - The distance outside of the kicking range from which neither the practitioner nor the assailant can touch the other.

No Holds Barred Competition (NHB) – A sport competition with few rules.

Non telegraphic Movement - Body mechanics or movements that do not inform an assailant of your intentions.

O

Offense - The armed and unarmed means and methods of attacking a criminal assailant.

Offensive Flow - Continuous offensive movements (kicks, blows, and strikes) with unbroken continuity that ultimately neutralize or terminate the opponent. (See compound attack.)

Offensive Reaction Time (ORT) - The elapsed time between target selection and target impaction.

P

Pain Tolerance - Your ability to physically and psychologically withstand pain.

Parry - A defensive technique; a quick, forceful slap that redirects an assailant's linear attack. There are two types of parries: horizontal and vertical.

Patience - A combative attribute. The ability to endure and tolerate difficulty.

Perception - Interpretation of vital information acquired from your senses when faced with a potentially threatening situation.

Physical Attributes - The numerous physical qualities that enhance your combative skills and abilities.

Physical Component - One of the three vital components of the CFA system. The physical component includes the physical aspects of fighting including Physical Fitness, Weapon/Technique Mastery, and Combative Attributes. (See mental component and spiritual component.)

Physical Conditioning - (See combative fitness.)

Physical Fitness - (See combative fitness.)

Positioning - The spatial relationship of the assailant to the assailed person in terms of target exposure, escape, angle of attack, and various other strategic considerations.

Power - A physical attribute of armed and unarmed combat. The amount of force you can generate when striking an anatomical target.

Power Generators – Specific points on your body which generate impact power. There are three anatomical power generators: shoulders, hips, and feet.

Precision - (See accuracy.)

Preparedness – A state of being ready for combat. There are three components of preparedness: affective preparedness, cognitive preparedness and psychomotor preparedness.

Proficiency Training - A CFA training methodology requiring the practitioner to execute a specific body weapon, technique, maneuver or tactic over and over for a prescribed number or repetitions. (See conditioning training and street training.)

Proxemics - The study of the nature and effect of man's personal space.

Proximity - The ability to maintain a strategically safe distance from a threatening individual.

Psychological Conditioning - The process of conditioning the mind for the horrors and rigors of real combat.

Punch - A quick, forceful strike of the fists.

Punching Range - One of the three ranges of unarmed combat. Punching range is the mid range of unarmed combat from which the fighter uses his hands to strike his assailant. (See kicking range and grappling range.)

Punching Range Tools - The various body weapons that are employed in the punching range of unarmed combat, including finger jabs, palm heel strikes, rear cross, knife hand strikes, horizontal and shovel hooks, uppercuts, and hammer fist strikes. (See grappling range tools and kicking range tools.)

Q

Qualities of Combat - (See attributes of combat.)

R

Range - The spatial relationship between a fighter and a threatening assailant.

Range Deficiency - The inability to effectively fight and defend in all ranges (armed and unarmed) of combat.

Range Manipulation - A combative attribute. The strategic manipulation of combat ranges.

Range Proficiency - A combative attribute. The ability to effectively fight and defend in all ranges (armed and unarmed) of combat.

Ranges of Engagement - (See combat ranges.)

Ranges of Unarmed Combat - The three distances a fighter might physically engage with an assailant while involved in unarmed combat: kicking range, punching range, and grappling range.

Raze – To level, demolish or obliterate.

Razer – One who performs the Razing methodology.

Razing – The second phase of the WidowMaker Program. A series of vicious close quarter techniques designed to physically and psychologically extirpate a criminal attacker.

Reaction Dynamics - The assailant's physical response or reaction to a particular tool, technique, or weapon after initial contact is made.

Reaction Time - The elapsed time between a stimulus and the response to that particular stimulus (See offensive reaction time and defensive reaction time.)

Rear Cross - A straight punch delivered from the rear hand that crosses from right to left (if in a left stance) or left to right (if in a right stance).

Rear Side - The side of the body furthest from the assailant (See lead side.)

Refinement - The strategic and methodical process of improving or perfecting.

Repetition - Performing a single movement, exercise, strike or action continuously for a specific period.

Rhythm - Movements characterized by the natural ebb and flow of related elements.

S

Safety - One of the three criteria for a CFA body weapon, technique, maneuver or tactic. It means the that the tool, technique, maneuver or tactic provides the least amount of danger and risk for the practitioner (See efficiency and effectiveness.)

Self-Confidence - Having trust and faith in yourself.

Set - A term used to describe a grouping of repetitions.

Shadow Fighting - A CFA training exercise used to develop and refine your tools, techniques, and attributes of armed and unarmed combat.

Skeletal Alignment - The proper alignment or arrangement of your body. Skeletal Alignment maximizes the structural integrity of striking tools.

Skills – One of the three factors that determine who will win a street fight. Skills refers to psychomotor proficiency with the tools and techniques of combat. (See Attitude and Knowledge.)

Slipping - A defensive maneuver that permits you to avoid an assailant's linear blow without stepping out of range. Slipping can be accomplished by quickly snapping the head and upper torso sideways (right or left) to avoid the blow.

Snap Back - A defensive maneuver that permits you to avoid an assailant's linear and circular blow without stepping out of range. The snap back can be accomplished by quickly snapping the head backwards to avoid the assailant's blow.

Sparring – A training exercise where two (or more) fighters fight each other while wearing protective equipment.

Speed - A physical attribute of armed and unarmed combat. The rate or a measure of the rapid rate of motion.

Spiritual Component - One of the three vital components of the CFA system. The spiritual component includes the metaphysical issues and aspects of existence (See physical component and mental component.)

Sport Oriented Training – Training that is geared for competition that is governed by a set of rules. (See combat oriented training and ritual oriented training.)

Sprawling – A grappling technique used to counter a double or single leg takedown.

Square-Off - To be face-to-face with the body opponent bag.

Stance - One of the many strategic postures that you assume prior to or during armed or unarmed combat.

Strategic/Tactical development - One of the five elements of CFA's mental component.

Strategy - A carefully planned method of achieving your goal of engaging an assailant under advantageous conditions.

Street Fight - A spontaneous and violent confrontation between two or more individuals wherein no rules apply.

Street Fighter - An unorthodox combatant who has no formal training. His combative skills and tactics are usually developed in the street by the process of trial and error.

Street Training - A CFA training methodology requiring the practitioner to deliver explosive compound attacks for ten to twenty-seconds (See conditioning training and proficiency training.)

Strength Training - The process of developing muscular strength through systematic application of progressive resistance.

Striking Art - A combat art that relies predominantly on striking techniques to neutralize or terminate a criminal attacker.

Striking Tool - A natural body weapon that impacts with the assailant's anatomical target.

Strong Side - The strongest and most coordinated side of your body.

Structure - A definite and organized pattern.

Style - The distinct manner in which a fighter executes or performs his combat skills.

Stylistic Integration - The purposeful and scientific collection of tools and techniques from various disciplines, which are strategically integrated and dramatically altered to meet three essential criteria: efficiency, effectiveness, and combative safety.

Submission Hold – (also known as control and restraint techniques). Many of the locks and holds that create sufficient pain to cause the adversary to submit.

Submission Technique - Includes all locks, bars, and holds that cause sufficient pain to cause the adversary to submit.

System - The unification of principles, philosophies, rules, strategies, methodologies, tools, and techniques or a particular method of combat.

T

Tactic - The skill of using the available means to achieve an end.

Target Awareness - A combative attribute which encompasses 5 strategic principles: target orientation, target recognition, target selection, target impaction, and target exploitation.

Target Exploitation - A combative attribute. The strategic maximization of your assailant's reaction dynamics during a fight. Target Exploitation can be applied in both armed and unarmed encounters.

Target Impaction - The successful striking of the appropriate anatomical target.

Target Orientation - A combative attribute. Having a workable knowledge of the assailant's anatomical targets.

Target Recognition - The ability to immediately recognize appropriate anatomical targets during an emergency self-defense situation.

Target Selection - The process of mentally selecting the appropriate anatomical target for your self-defense situation. This is predicated on certain factors, including proper force response, assailant's positioning and range.

Technique - A systematic procedure by which a task is accomplished.

Telegraphing - Unintentionally making your intentions known to your adversary.

Tempo - The speed or rate at which you speak.

Timing - A physical and mental attribute or armed and unarmed combat. Your ability to execute a movement at the optimum moment.

Tool - (See body weapon.)

Traditional Martial Arts - Any martial art that fails to evolve and change to meet the demands and characteristics of its present environment.

Traditional Style/System - (See traditional martial art.)

Training Drills - The various exercises and drills aimed at perfecting combat skills, attributes, and tactics.

U

Unified Mind - A mind free and clear of distractions and focused on the combative situation.

Use of Force Response - A combative attribute. Selecting the appropriate level of force for a particular emergency self-defense situation.

V

Visualization – Also known as Mental Visualization or Mental Imagery. The purposeful formation of mental images and scenarios in the mind's eye.

W

Warm-up - A series of mild exercises, stretches, and movement designed to prepare you for more intense exercise.

Weak Side - The weakest and most uncoordinated side of your body.

Weapon and Technique Mastery - A component of CFA's physical component. The kinesthetic and psychomotor development of a weapon or combative technique.

Webbing - A reinforced palm heel strike primarily delivered to the assailant's chin. It is termed Webbing because your hands resemble a large web that wraps around the enemy's face.

WidowMaker Program – A fighting style created by Sammy Franco that is specifically designed to teach the law-abiding citizen how to use extreme force when faced with immediate threat of unlawful deadly criminal attack. The WidowMaker program is divided into two sections or phases: Webbing and Razing.

Y

Yell - A loud and aggressive scream or shout used for various strategic reasons.

Z

Zero Beat – One of the four beat classifications of the WidowMaker Program. Zero beat strikes are full pressure techniques applied to a specific target until it completely ruptures. Zero beat tools include gouging, biting and choking techniques

Zone One - Anatomical targets related to your senses, including the eyes, temple, nose, chin, and back of neck.

Zone Three - Anatomical targets related to your mobility, including thighs, knees, shins, and instep.

Zone Two - Anatomical targets related to your breathing, including front of neck, solar plexus, ribs, and groin.

About the Author

Sammy Franco is one of the world's foremost authorities on armed and unarmed combat. Highly regarded as a leading innovator in combat sciences, Mr. Franco was one of the premier pioneers in the field of "reality-based" self-defense and martial arts instruction.

Convinced of the limited usefulness of martial arts in real street fighting situations, Mr. Franco believes in the theory that the best way to change traditional thinking is to make antiquated ideas obsolete through superior methodology. His innovative ideas have made a significant contribution to changing the thinking of many in the field about how people can best defend themselves against vicious and formidable adversaries.

Sammy Franco is perhaps best known as the founder and creator of Contemporary Fighting Arts (CFA), a state-of-the-art offensive-based combat system that is specifically designed for real-world self-defense. CFA is a sophisticated and practical system of self-defense, designed specifically to provide efficient and effective methods to avoid, defuse, confront, and neutralize both armed and unarmed attackers.

After studying and training in numerous martial art systems and related disciplines and acquiring extensive firsthand experience from real "street" combat, Mr. Franco developed his first system, known as Analytical Street Fighting. This system, which was one of the first practical "street fighting" martial arts, employed an unrestrained reality-based training methodology known as Simulated Street Fighting. Analytical Street Fighting served as the foundation for the fundamental principles of Contemporary Fighting Arts and Mr. Franco's teaching methodology.

CFA also draws from the concepts and principles of numerous sciences and disciplines, including police and military science, criminal justice, criminology, sociology, human psychology, philosophy, histrionics, kinesics, proxemics, kinesiology, emergency medicine, crisis management, and human anatomy.

Sammy Franco has frequently been featured in martial art magazines, newspapers, and appeared on numerous radio and television programs. Mr. Franco has also authored numerous books, magazine articles and editorials, and has developed a popular library of instructional DVDs and workout music. As a matter of fact, his book Street Lethal was one of the first books ever published on the subject of reality based self-defense. His other books include Killer Instinct, When Seconds Count, 1001 Street Fighting Secrets, First Strike, The Bigger They Are – The Harder They Fall, War Machine, War Craft, Ground War, Warrior Wisdom, Out of the Cage, Gun Safety Handbook and Heavy Bag Training.

Sammy Franco's experience and credibility in the combat science is unequaled. One of his many accomplishments in this field includes the fact that he has earned the ranking of a Law Enforcement Master Instructor, and has designed, implemented, and taught officer survival

197

training to the United States Border Patrol (USBP). He instructs members of the US Secret Service, Military Special Forces, Washington DC Police Department, Montgomery County, Maryland Deputy Sheriffs, and the US Library of Congress Police. Sammy Franco is also a member of the prestigious International Law Enforcement Educators and Trainers Association (ILEETA) as well as the American Society of Law Enforcement Trainers (ASLET) and he is listed in the "Who's Who Director of Law Enforcement Instructors."

Sammy Franco is a nationally certified Law Enforcement Instructor in the following curricula: PR-24 Side-Handle Baton, Police Arrest and Control Procedures, Police Personal Weapons Tactics, Police Power Handcuffing Methods, Police Oleoresin Capsicum Aerosol Training (OCAT), Police Weapon Retention and Disarming Methods, Police Edged Weapon Countermeasures and "Use of Force" Assessment and Response Methods.

Mr. Franco is also a National Rifle Association (NRA) instructor who specializes in firearm safety, personal protection and advanced combat pistol shooting.

Mr. Franco holds a Bachelor of Arts degree in Criminal Justice from the University of Maryland. He is a regularly featured speaker at a number of professional conferences, and conducts dynamic and enlightening seminars on numerous aspects of self-defense and personal protection.

Mr. Franco has instructed thousands of students in his career, including instruction on street fighting, grappling and ground fighting, boxing and kick boxing, knife combat, multiple opponent survival skills, stick fighting, and firearms training. Having lived through street violence himself, Mr. Franco's goal is not its glorification, but to help people free themselves from violence and its costly price.

For more information about Mr. Franco and his unique Contemporary Fighting Arts system, you can visit his website at: www.sammyfranco.com

~Finis~

Made in the USA
Monee, IL
12 December 2020